SUCCESS TRAP

DR. STAN J. KATZ *and* AIMEE E. LIU

▼

SUCCESS TRAP

▲

Rethink
Your Ambitions
to Achieve
Greater Personal
and Professional
Fulfillment

Ticknor & Fields
New York 1990

For information about permission to reproduce selections
from this book, write to Permissions, Ticknor & Fields,
215 Park Avenue South, New York, New York 10003.

Library of Congress Cataloging-in-Publication Data

Katz, Stan J.
Success trap : rethink your ambitions to achieve greater personal
and professional fulfillment / Stan J. Katz and Aimee E. Liu.
p.   cm.
ISBN 0-89919-855-4
1. Success — Psychological aspects.   2. Goal (Psychology)   3. Self-
actualization (Psychology)   4. Conduct of life.   I. Liu, Aimee E.
II. Title.
BF637.S8K378   1990   89-20246
158'.1 — dc20   CIP

Printed in the United States of America

Q 10 9 8 7 6 5 4 3 2 1

To A. V. Katz, a truly successful man

S. K.

*To Marc, in the hope that he will one day
recognize how truly successful he is*

A. L.

ACKNOWLEDGMENTS

Once again we extend our thanks to Katrina Kenison, for sticking with us *almost* to the end of round two and for breathing life into this project through her own example. We also owe an enormous debt of gratitude to Caroline Sutton, for stepping in at the eleventh hour to shape and shepherd this book through its final stages, and to Gerry Morse, our manuscript editor, for her care and thoroughness.

Richard Pine continues to lend us that vital encouragement, advice, and most of all, conviction in our ability that keep us on track when we start to wander, for which we thank him. Arthur Pine and Lori Andiman, too, have taken a special interest in our work, which we greatly appreciate.

And to our families, especially Debra and Marty, we acknowledge that we would not be the authors — or people — we are without your enduring love and support. This book is yours as well as ours.

CONTENTS

Acknowledgments   vii
Preface   xi
Introduction   xiii

▼

I. THE CURSE OF UPWARD MOBILITY

1. Confronting the Edge of Success   3
   Your Success Profile   18
2. Measuring the Obsession   23
   Confront Your Own Obsessions   47

▼

II. THE PUSH TO BE SOMEBODY

3. Learning to Strive   53
   Create a History of Your Success Conditioning 69
4. Training for the Competition   71
   What's Your Competition Quotient?   101
5. The Push to Specialize   106
   Does Your Specialty Suit You?   127

▼

III. THE PRICE OF GLORY

6. Success as a Habit   131
   Chart Your Success Milestones   156

CONTENTS

7. Success and the Gender Gap   158
    Choosing the Right Career: A Plan   178
    Your Sex Role Inventory   181

▼

IV. TOWARD A NEW PHILOSOPHY
OF SUCCESS

8. For Love *and* Money: Toward a New Definition
    of Success   185
9. Learning to Thrive: The Integrated Life   204
10. Beyond Ambition: Making a Career of Life   228

    Notes   247

PREFACE

While this book is not intended to be used as a manual for success, it does contain questions and suggestions that can help you reassess your goals and values and develop a personally meaningful definition of success. Each chapter contains thought-provoking exercises to help you clarify your own personal attitudes, beliefs, and priorities. For this reason, you may want to keep pencil and paper at hand as you read.

You will also find numerous case histories of individuals who have discovered just how difficult it is to negotiate that edge between external ambition and internal collapse. These cases are drawn from actual clinical practice. Some are composites, while others describe specific patients, but all names and identifying details have been changed to protect the individuals' privacy.

INTRODUCTION

We all want to be "successful." The goal of material achievement is drilled into us by family, society, and the media. Parents urge their children to work hard so they can be "somebody." Academia continues the pressure with competitive scores and rewards for standout performers. Bookstores are loaded with manuals instructing readers how to get to the top of their fields, make lots of money, and accumulate power — tacitly suggesting, if not openly stating, that these are the goals that should drive every red-blooded American. Magazine headlines boldly promise shortcuts to success, and cover photos glamorize the rich and famous as prototypes for the "successful" life.

At the same time, we are exhorted to be independent and individualistic. For all the lip service paid to family values and charity at home, the trend among young adults — the baby boomers — in this country for the past two decades has been to embrace a brand of self-sufficiency that often crosses the line into utter selfishness. Tom Wolfe called it the "me" generation, Christopher Lasch, the age of narcissism, and Philip Slater, the pursuit of loneliness. Whatever we call it, this generation's egoism has had a pernicious effect on society. Divorce and suicide rates, violence, environmental destruction, and white-collar crime have been climbing steadily. At the individual level, the rate of emotional depression over the last two generations has multiplied *tenfold!*[1] Men and women between the ages of twenty-five and forty-four report the highest rate of depression; in some major cities as many as 10 percent in this age group have experienced a serious depressive episode. Although the rates of depression and attempted suicide among women are two to four times higher than those among men, the effective suicide rate is four times higher for men, proving that both sexes are vulnerable to the deep and growing alienation in our culture.

The sources of this alienation are our cultural passion for individualism — often pursued at the expense of institutions such as religion, family, and government — and our soaring, often unattainable expectations. We are setting ourselves up for failure by targeting stratospheric goals while rejecting the social and emotional safety nets that could save us when we fall back to earth.

In this culture, if you're not aggressively self-sufficient and achievement-oriented, you're made to feel that you're out of step. But for all the hype extolling the various external images of success, can you explain to your own satisfaction *why* you should embrace these images as personal goals? Surprisingly few people can.

When I ask my patients how they would like to be eulogized when they die, most reply that they want to be remembered as a good person, parent, spouse, and friend. Having a huge net worth, a prestigious title, or control over a corporate empire are rarely even mentioned in the final analysis. Yet these are the very goals that dominate the lives of many of the same people, often at the expense of their families and friends, who they *know* are more important. There is an enormous gap between the stated values in our society and the way most of us actually lead our lives.

In some cases this conflict between external and internal priorities indicates deeper uncertainty over the human condition. If you question the intrinsic meaning of life and worry about being forgotten in death, ambition can serve as a subconscious shield. On one level, it provides distraction: the more energy you invest in your accomplishments, the less you can spare to worry about death. On another, it holds out the prospect of immortality: if you are famous, wealthy, or prestigious, more people are likely to remember you after you're gone. Just as the goal of making one's mark can inject a sense of purpose into life, the prospect of lasting recognition can make death somewhat less frightening, but the subconscious attempt to dodge mortality places such a high premium on outward success that it tends to overshadow other human needs and desires.

Success in today's world is usually defined by the superficial rewards glorified in the media: wealth, power, fame, luxury, and prestige. What's lacking are the internal benchmarks of fulfillment. Few among us have a firm idea of what it takes to truly feel successful — not just to achieve but to thrive. It's easy for an outsider to say that a woman who has risen to top management of a major corporation and earns nearly a million dollars a year is successful, but would the woman agree? That depends largely on the sacrifices she's made to get to the top, the quality of her life outside work, and — perhaps most important of all — her personal reasons for pursuing her particular career. If she has a positive sense of direction that encompasses her whole life, not just her professional career or bankbook, and if she understands why she wants what she wants, her accomplishments may give her genuine satisfaction, making her a success in her own eyes. However, if she does not have this clarity of purpose, and especially if she has been struggling to live up to someone else's definition of success — a parent's, a husband's, or perhaps society's — she is likely to reach the top of her professional ladder but wonder why she feels so dissatisfied. Standing at the edge of success and confronting the uncertainty that lies beyond, she begins to realize that her identity as an individual has been compromised by the forces pushing her to attain career stardom. She has become trapped by the pressure to get ahead, and her life is out of balance. Persuaded that professional advancement is what she *should* want, she has lost sight of the elements that would truly bring her fulfillment.

Even if we realize that the rise to material wealth and prominence can be grueling and painful, and that our family and friends deserve priority in our lives, we still may unwittingly be drawn in by the mystique of success that permeates American culture. As children, most of us came to believe that academic, professional, and financial achievement are good, and any kind of failure is bad. The inevitable conclusion was that winning brings happiness and losing means misery — and the middle zone is pure frustration. Depending on how you were raised and treated, you came to expect that you would land in one of these strata, but whatever your expectations, you *hoped* for success.

If you came from a privileged family, you may have assumed that those privileges would extend to you automatically, or you may have felt obligated to prove your worth by earning outside recognition on your own. If people said you were unusually talented or smart, you may have felt pressured to live up to this specialness by achieving professional or artistic acclaim. Even if you viewed yourself as a failure, you still inevitably hoped that one day you would be deemed a success at something, and thereby acquire self-worth. The terms of achievement handed down, however, are always outer directed. Most of us assume that we can be successful only if others call us successful. And it is usually taken for granted that once we've been so labeled, we will automatically be a success in our own eyes as well.

In childhood it's natural to accept the prescribed terms of success that are set down by your immediate family and community. You learn what it takes to prove yourself, and the approval your achievements win from parents and friends genuinely feels good — so good, in fact, that you eagerly strive to chalk up more kudos. But the desire to achieve too often turns into a compulsion to overachieve, especially among youngsters who receive approval *only* when they succeed in objective tasks or challenges and are generally ignored or criticized when they are not out-performing their peers. Of course, since superiority is the standard for praise and advancement in our educational system, all youngsters are vulnerable to some extent. Those who fail to measure up to the success standards of parents or teachers may turn to alternative role models, gangs, whose standards seem more attainable.

Ironically, as the premium placed on achievement escalates in high school, college, and early adulthood, objective accomplishments may provide little real pleasure and create anxiety. The competition of peers increases dramatically as the pressure builds to choose a field, narrow your focus, specialize. Instead of encouraging the pursuit of a varied life with multiple options, interests, and goals, the American success model champions single-mindedness, and young people are pushed to select a profession and embark on a career before they are old enough to vote, much less experience working life firsthand. As a result, career choices tend to be made not because a student has a flair for a particular job, loves the work, or yearns to understand the inner workings of a particular profession, but because *other people* have exerted some compelling pressure or opened doors in a particular direction. A college senior decides to go into publishing because it seems like a logical career for an English major and she doesn't know what else to do. A math major goes into computer technology because his father can pull strings at IBM. A political science major drops out of school to get married and takes a job as a secretary to support her husband through law school. These choices will shape these individuals' identities and definitions of success in the years to come, yet they are not choices of the heart. When critical career decisions are based on convenience, coincidence, imitation, and economic urgency rather than on aptitude or passion, it's little wonder that later career success fails to bring the desired personal fulfillment.

Given the emphasis on upward mobility in this culture, most

of us struggle determinedly to be Somebody, with all the material rewards that exalted status promises. But it is important to distinguish between the wonderful things material success can buy and the heavy price it can exact. If you ignore the dangers to your personal sense of worth and well-being — or believe you are immune to them — you may eventually find yourself in a crisis from which it is difficult to recover. Suddenly questioning why you're so driven, why you've made the choices and sacrifices that have shaped your private and professional life thus far, you may wonder if there's any way to restore harmony to your existence. Is it too late to strike out in an entirely different direction? Can you stop your fantasies of future success from sabotaging your life? Can you redefine your marriage or relationship, renew your children's trust and affection, and begin again to pursue interests that genuinely matter to you? Can you even remember what these interests are? And can you recall the personal goals that motivated you before external success became your life's ambition? The answer is yes, if you have the courage to trust yourself.

To begin, you will need to look back and trace the origins of your own assumptions about success. Then you will need to create your personal definition of success, encompassing not only your career and finances but also your family, friendships, personal health, and spiritual, intellectual, and emotional growth. Through a balanced approach that focuses more on personal than competitive excellence, it is possible to achieve the goals you deem most important without sacrificing too much. Finally, you may need to make some changes in the way you live, the way you see, the way you think, the way you relate to others, and most important of all, the way you perceive yourself. Whether or not you accumulate fame or fortune, as you build confidence in your *internal* success, you will feel more complete as an individual and more connected to the world around you.

▼

PART I

THE CURSE OF
UPWARD MOBILITY

1

▼

CONFRONTING THE EDGE OF SUCCESS

*For what is a man advantaged, if he gain the whole world,
and lose himself, or be cast away?*

— *Luke 9:25*

IT WAS 10:00 P.M. and the law office was deserted, except for
the security guard and somebody moaning in one of the outer
offices. Another after-hours rendezvous, the guard thought,
smiling to himself. But then the moan turned to a scream for
help. This was not arousal but pain. Pushing the door open, the
guard found Michael Kaufmann, a thirty-nine-year-old associate, doubled over and clutching his chest.

"Call the ambulance," Michael gasped. "Heart attack!" As the
guard grabbed the phone, a new paroxysm of pain and dizzi-
ness sent Michael tumbling off his chair. Reaching in vain to
steady himself, he clutched the stack of contracts that had kept
him working late. In that instant, it hit him: these and all the
other pieces of paper that comprised his career might very well
be killing him. If he should die tonight, he would have sacrificed

3

everything in pursuit of a success built on clauses and conditions — and he would have failed, at that.

In the hours and days that followed, as he submitted to the tests and therapies that would pull him back from the edge of death, Michael saw himself moving closer to another edge — the edge of success. The approach tilted upward so that he couldn't really see to the other side, but he had the vivid impression that when he reached the brink, as it seemed inevitable he would, he would fall, headlong and helpless, into a great black emptiness that might well be never-ending.

The more Michael's doctors did to preserve his life, the more determined he became to prevent his fall into darkness. Questioning the choices and values that had shaped his ambitions to this point, he realized that because at age twenty-five he had eagerly embraced the terms of a career that might one day propel him into a partnership at a prestigious law firm, he had never allowed himself to look in any direction but forward. As long as he kept his eye on the prize, he believed, he would keep moving toward it and past his competitors. But in the process, he had lost almost everything that once gave meaning to his life. He'd struggled for years to maintain both a relationship and his career, but the demands of his work, both on his energy and his time, left little for his girlfriend, and eventually she left him. He missed the closeness he'd once had with his parents and brother, but though he frequently planned to visit them, his work almost always seemed to intervene. The only people he saw regularly were his coworkers, but the competitive atmosphere prohibited any real camaraderie or trust among them. It wasn't surprising, he reflected, that he had lost his sense of humor and fun along with his old friends. He had even had to give away his beloved golden retriever because he didn't have time to provide the care and attention the dog required.

Not only had Michael's career diminished the quality of his life, it had taken a real toll on his health, possibly contributing to his heart attack. His sixty-hour workweek permitted no time for hobbies, outside interests, or regular exercise. He made dates to play tennis but often had to break them to tend to crises at the office. The same thing happened whenever he scheduled a medical checkup, and as a result he hadn't had one in more than five years. Meanwhile, the relentless grind of work contributed to his increased smoking — up to nearly a pack a day. And when he got home, he often needed a couple of scotches to unwind. On his rare days off he was usually so exhausted that he just stayed in bed.

Yet Michael had never allowed himself any regrets. His $95,000 salary and $300,000 condominium, his parents' pride, and the occasional encouragement and praise he received from his superiors had convinced him that he was on his way to success. Nearly losing his life, however, made him suddenly and painfully aware of its emptiness.

The near miss forced Michael to start analyzing why he drove himself so hard. His first inclination was to find a scapegoat. His boss was too demanding. His parents had always expected great things of him. His teachers and professors had directed him into law. His girlfriend had pushed him to make a lot of money so they could get married and have kids. Day after day he searched for someone to blame without acknowledging that he himself, with his illusions about achievement, was the real culprit. For it was he who had finally embraced material wealth and position as personal goals, almost to the exclusion of all others. It was he who, until his heart attack, had been convinced that the payoff for all his hard work — becoming a partner — would make him happy.

Now Michael wondered if he could ever be truly happy, and he realized too that he had no idea what it would take to make him a genuine success in his own eyes. Faced with the suddenly terrifying uncertainty of his future, an uncertainty that he had carefully shrouded in single-minded ambition, he felt at once desperate and bewildered.

Michael's predicament is not unique to lawyers, or even to

this century. Aristotle and his predecessors contemplated the perils of ambition long before anyone ever heard the terms "fast track," "burnout," or "winning edge." Issues of mortality, fulfillment, and compensation — indeed, the meaning of life — have been the stuff of philosophy since civilization began, and probably will continue to be until the bitter end. But these issues are particularly germane in today's America, where competition has been raised to a national obsession and career "success" to an almost mandatory personal priority. Not to be competitive in this culture is equated with being a wimp, and not striving to be successful is called copping out. Yet for all our ambition, few among us ever stop to develop a personal and meaningful definition of success that allows us to thrive as well as strive. Instead, we absorb a composite of largely superficial illusions from the media, parental pressures, and peer aspirations.

The lure of success is not limited to careerists. Marcia Bowden never had any intention of achieving professional glory, but her dreams of making it to the top were every bit as potent — and destructive — as Michael's. Marcia's vision of success had been shaped by her mother and father, Polish immigrants who ran a corner candy store, and by her lower-middle-class childhood in Chicago. To get married and have two children and a house of her own were the goals that defined success for her. So, to her parents' delight, she married the wealthiest boy in her high school. Having long since discarded any thought of going on to college or developing her own considerable talents as a writer, she stood by her husband loyally as he moved up through the ranks of his father's firm. She produced two healthy children and turned their sprawling suburban home into an immaculate showcase.

Marcia's mother was enormously proud of her daughter's accomplishments. Marcia's friends envied her lifestyle. No one was allowed to penetrate the facade far enough to see how unhappy

Marcia and her family really were. Not even her mother knew how tyrannically Marcia's husband treated her and the children. He was the executive in charge of absolutely everything, from the family purse to the course of discipline the children received when their grades fell below B. Whenever Marcia's personal opinions or obligations conflicted with his, it was understood that she, not he, must make the necessary adjustments. Beneath the seamless exterior, Marcia's life was in tatters. Her children, who were beyond her control, expressed their confusion through Patty's general surliness and violent tantrums and Timmy's bed wetting at age eight. Marcia derived little real pleasure from her material possessions and surroundings, and she felt isolated, unable to confide in anyone for fear it would get back to her husband and cause severe reprisals. Her self-esteem was almost nonexistent. Even with everything she'd ever thought necessary for success, she felt like an abject failure.

Keeping Your Eye on the Prize

To succeed in this culture is to become what everyone else tells you you're supposed to be. It is assumed, almost as an after-thought, that when you get there you'll magically be happy. But as both Michael and Marcia discovered, this formula leaves little room for genuine personal fulfillment in the here and now. Quite the opposite, it often undermines any source of fulfillment that is not related to the climb. Conversely, it tells you that if you hate what you're doing but appear successful to others, you would be a fool to change. Not surprisingly, then, when this quest for success dominates everyday life year after year, each step up the ladder brings less true satisfaction and more anxiety. At some point a crisis is inevitable, whether or not the rewards of fame, fortune, and power are ever realized. This crisis exposes the edge of success: *that line where external success and internal collapse coincide.*

Of course, few of us consciously choose to close out our options and compromise our happiness, but it is understood that a certain amount of sacrifice is necessary to get ahead. A child may entertain the possibility of having multiple roles, passions, and dreams in life, but in adulthood too much diversity is frowned upon. Grown people who actively pursue multiple and varied ambitions, interests, and activities are generally accused of spreading themselves too thin or, worse, condescendingly called dilettantes. America's emphasis on competition and specialization has precluded the possibility of a Renaissance-style career for most of us. Instead, we are subtly but effectively conditioned to be single-minded — to name our ambition and "go for it."

Not only is there a strong bias against tangential enterprises, but there is an assumed conflict between personal and professional life, which often forces the upwardly mobile to choose between the two spheres. Many women still routinely surrender or indefinitely postpone their own career aspirations in order to acquire success secondhand through their partners. Those who choose to make their own professional success often put their personal lives on hold, or else feel brutally torn between career and family priorities. Many researchers believe that this conflict is to blame for the higher incidence of depression among women.

Even men, who traditionally relied on supportive wives to help them up the professional ladder, are just as likely to view marriage as a conflicting commitment. "I don't imagine I'll have time for a serious relationship while I'm getting my career established," said a recent business school graduate. "But if I stick with my ten-year plan, I should be in a position to get married and start a family when I'm around thirty-five." Even the best-laid plans can go awry, however, especially when career concerns are allowed to overshadow everything else for so long. By age thirty-five, this MBA may have lost many of the personal qualities needed for marriage and parenthood. Developing a satisfying relationship and family life is a long-term process that requires commitment, trust, and understanding, qualities that cannot simply be mandated by executive fiat.

At the same time, if you view both your professional and your private lives as arenas where you must surpass external standards of performance, you probably will end up feeling thoroughly frustrated. Balancing your life does not simply mean adding new layers of commitment, though the conflicting demands of home and work sometimes make it seem that this is the case. In fact, balancing your life means reducing superficial obligations on all sides and integrating personally important relationships and pursuits with professional goals.

This may involve shifting from the formal socializing you've always resented to social events that include your family and that you enjoy. It may mean that you forget about decorating the nursery and spend that time playing with your newborn. Or it may simply be a matter of giving yourself permission to follow your instincts — to relax when you're exhausted, to spend time with your son when he needs you instead of when your schedule permits, to daydream or read a novel instead of fighting to maintain a rigid work schedule. In short, to balance your life, you first need to identify and weed out those goals and activities that support a purely external image of success, and nurture those that support your personal terms of fulfillment.

This can be especially difficult if you have a high-powered career, since many professions presume total dedication as a prerequisite for advancement. Out of this presumption has grown the myth of quality time, in which marital, social, and family relationships are pigeonholed into token moments, while Career, with a capital C, is the centerpiece around which all else revolves. Because our culture equates economic and professional success with continual upward movement, we dare not allow ourselves to muse, play, or just stand still when the mood strikes. Such impulses must be channeled into "constructive" activities, which in turn must be scheduled around career priorities.

Time, after all, is money, and the rate of exchange is constantly escalating. The average workweek increased from 40.6 hours to 46.8 hours between 1973 and 1987, while the average worker's leisure time decreased from 26.2 hours to 16.2 hours per week. Professionals, small-business owners, and executives put in up to 65 hours per week.[1] And employed women, who are still expected to bear the lion's share of housework and child care in addition to their job responsibilities, work longest of all — up to 15 hours a week more than either men or nonemployed women.[2] With the addition of "efficiency-increasing" devices, such as cellular phones, beepers, dictating machines, laptop computers, and nationwide business clubs, the business of work seems to be eclipsing the business of life.

There are numerous reasons for this escalating pace. Increasing competition in the marketplace has pushed employers to demand greater efficiency. Technological advancements have made greater efficiency possible and therefore have raised productivity standards. Economic strains have necessitated budget cuts, which have caused massive layoffs in many firms, which in turn have pressured those who remain to fill in the gaps. Finally, changes in the balance of foreign trade have caused a general shift in the United States from a manufacturing to a service economy based on billable hours.

Despite the increasing pressure in the workplace, numerous management studies have proved that total dedication does *not* enhance job performance. On the contrary, without a fulfilling personal life you may well get less out of your career, not more, and without a significant identity outside the home you will probably be a less confident spouse and parent.

One project that suggests a direct connection between personal well-being and professional fulfillment is the Grant Study of Adult Development at Harvard University, which has tracked the lives and careers of 268 men chosen from Harvard College's classes of 1939 through 1944. Those graduates who became company presidents also ended up with the stablest marriages, the deepest friendships, and the most moderate lifestyles. Dr. George Vaillant, director of the ongoing study, explains: "There's no question that conventional lives statistically are the happiest. Stopping smoking, exercising, working hard, eating breakfast, and not getting divorced — all these humdrum things correlate directly with happiness."[3] If, instead of cultivating a "conventional" life, you invest so much in one direction that you have few other avenues for gratification, you may well lose at home *and* at work.

Extrinsic versus Intrinsic Motivation

One critical distinction here is between what psychologists call extrinsic and intrinsic motivation. Extrinsic motivation nudges us to view work and sacrifice as the cost of money and perhaps status, while intrinsic motivation encourages us to enjoy both our work and life itself for their own sake. Extrinsic motivation provides an external rationale for work and tends to encourage competition; intrinsic motivation nurtures an internal rationale for work and encourages personal fulfillment. Extrinsic motivation is fueled by dissatisfaction, anxiety, and material desire, intrinsic motivation by passion and pride. Most of us respond to both types of motivation, but they are not interchangeable.

If you are driven primarily by extrinsic motivation you may have a surplus of ambition that prevents you from taking pleasure in the process or quality of your work as an end in itself. What matters most is the reward — the praise, the money, the power, or the recognition your efforts will earn. Even though your intense drive may keep you at your desk day and night, you may find it difficult to concentrate on the job at hand. Instead, much of your time may be spent analyzing office politics or the performance of your colleagues. You may become so preoccupied with measuring up that the quality of your own performance suffers.

Even in the competitive, high-stakes world of baseball, extrinsic motivation actually damages performance. Rumors leading up to a trade cause players to strive extra hard to boost their performance, but the records of fifty-nine players involved in midseason trades from 1964 to 1981 show that their batting averages dropped during the period preceding the trade. After the trade, when the players stopped trying so hard to win and just played the game, their batting performance rose by an average of thirty points, exceeding their three-year averages.[4]

If you are highly ambitious, you may find that your working hours lengthen, your friendships suffer, and you develop physical complaints as the years pass. In short, you endure a lot of hardships that cause you to feel martyred by your work. Unfortunately, personal suffering doesn't always buy professional success. If you've sacrificed your personal welfare and do not receive the anticipated recognition or advancement, you may feel crushed and resentful, and that will make it even more difficult to recover your balance.

Alternatively, if you have strong intrinsic motivation, you may so love your work that you don't much care whether others deem you a success. Because you appreciate the intrinsic value of your accomplishments, you don't depend on external praise or rewards. Because you're not driven by the need for external reinforcement, you are less likely to become preoccupied with competition and long-term strategizing. You may strive to find a personal challenge and interest even in tasks that do not at first seem particularly interesting. If you cannot muster any enthusiasm for your work, you may have a hard time following through, but if the interest is there, you may put in very long hours and push yourself to do the best job possible. When your primary motivation is intrinsic, you won't consider the time or effort a sacrifice, because you enjoy what you're doing. Also, because you value personal fulfillment, you will probably make room in your life for intimacy and relaxation, even if you *appear* to be a "workaholic."

You will undoubtedly see aspects of yourself in both descriptions, but you may not know which type of motivation is dominant. You may think you react to one type of motivation when your behavior and underlying aspirations actually suggest the other. This is understandable given our culture's mixed messages about achievement and the work ethic. As a society we are so quick to condemn blatant fame-and-fortune hunters that most of them eventually justify their pursuits in terms of leadership, creativity, or other socially laudable ambitions. People who truly love their work, on the other hand, are often pushed to adopt consumer values, confusing wealth and recognition with personal fulfillment.

Most of us unwittingly adjust our natural inclinations in order to fit the mainstream. Unfortunately, in doing so we may sacrifice what genuinely matters most. The young doctor who loves research is persuaded by her colleagues to join their lucrative practice; she quickly becomes accustomed to the high income but finds her daily routine exhausting and dull. The musician who earns a modest income through gigs in cabarets and occasional commercial work becomes convinced that he will never be respectable unless he gets a "real" job in business management, so he ends up with only slightly more money and a desk job that he finds stultifying. It's easy to make choices like these in the name of success, only to find that the detours you've taken are neither productive nor satisfying. Learning to block out the external pressures and discover what truly motivates you is an essential first step toward finding your own track.

External versus Internal Success

As you begin to consider the interplay of extrinsic and intrinsic motivation in your life, it's important to realize that there are two corresponding categories of success. Extrinsic motivation points you in the direction of external success, signaled by acquisition of wealth, power, adulation, prestige, or fame. Such success is determined by outsiders — colleagues, family, the public, or the media. Intrinsic motivation points you in the direction of internal success, signaled by high self-esteem, pride, and personal fulfillment, all of which can be determined only by you. External success rarely leads directly to internal success. More often, it creates an obstruction of guilt, anxiety, and pressure, which must be overcome before the two types of success can coexist peacefully. Internal success, however, creates the ideal conditions for external success to follow, and it frequently does.

When Michael had his heart attack he was forced to recognize the chasm between the internal and external achievements of his life. He was well paid, respected, and on his way to becoming a partner at an early age. On the surface, he had no reason to complain, and in fact he had been conditioned to feel guilty for not relishing his rewards. All his life he'd been led to believe that if his career was successful, he was successful. It took a brush with death to make him see how badly he'd been misled and how little these external accomplishments really meant to him. Worse still, the struggle for external success had dominated him for so long that he had lost his resources and his passion in other areas. He couldn't remember when he had last done something truly gratifying. He had no driving curiosity or interests. And he wasn't even sure he was capable of true love and intimacy anymore. Perched precariously on the edge of success, Michael saw personal fulfillment as an almost impossible dream.

Though she was in quite different circumstances, Marcia felt much the same kind of hopelessness as she surveyed her life. She had persisted in believing that material success and marital longevity would make her happy, yet by age twenty-eight she felt imprisoned. Despite her affluence, she had not a cent to call her own. For all the work she'd put into her children, her home, and her husband's career, she felt qualified for nothing outside her family. Even worse, she felt that she was in some way responsible for her husband's coldness and her children's emotional and behavioral problems. Having shouldered the responsibility for proving herself a success in the eyes of the world, she felt that her failure was her own fault, but she saw no way out.

Reading the Signs

Michael and Marcia were fortunate in one respect: they discovered the edge of success at a relatively early age, which gave them more time and more opportunities to turn their lives around. Disillusionment usually doesn't occur until middle age, by which time up-and-comers have risen through the ranks and watched enough of the competition fall away to recognize their own increasing isolation. They have felt the pressure of rising expectations — their own and those of their superiors. They have watched their personal lives suffer as a result of their careers. And they are increasingly conscious of time passing them by without bringing the anticipated fulfillment. Their years of sacrifice, loneliness, and false expectations have not prepared them to deal with the crisis of their success.

It's not always easy to read the signs. You may feel chronically harried and rushed, yet blame it on "the world today." You may feel that you never do as good a job as you would like, but reassure yourself that no one else does, either. You may wish you

15

lived in another place or had a different job, and fantasize about retiring early so you can realize your dreams. Or you may be so haunted by the thought of a debilitating catastrophe striking you in your prime, one that would force you to slow down and reevaluate your ambitions, that you drive yourself even harder to defy the premonition. Ignoring these warnings, however, may simply hasten the crisis.

When the telltale feelings of disenchantment and malaise begin to crop up, few of us recognize that ambition may be the cause. In our society, the outer trappings of material prosperity are viewed as a sacred good. It's acceptable to complain that your spouse is too demanding, your vacation too short, your children too unruly, or your bills too high, but complain that money, fame, or power is wrecking your life and people will think you're mad. While the myth persists that material success will make everything better, this type of success, or the quest for it, often is the real culprit. The surrounding problems are usually casualties rather than causes.

Ralph Waldo Emerson observed that the vision of success as the "sweet without the bitter" is nothing more than an illusion, and a dangerous one at that. "I do not wish more external goods," he wrote, "neither possessions, nor honors, nor power, nor persons. The gain is apparent; the tax is certain."[5] A century and a half later, Emerson's wisdom is as apt as ever, but our fantasies of success are, if anything, even more powerful. Particularly when we are young and impressionable, the apparent gains of external success may be so alluring that we voluntarily raise our ambitions and streamline our lives to feed those desires. But these fantasies almost never incorporate the taxes or real-life consequences of such a single-minded pursuit of material wealth and public recognition. Instead, they promise that the ends will justify virtually any means. As time passes and our hard work starts to pay off, we naturally feel a certain satisfaction in our accomplishments and may tend to overlook the price we pay. For reasons we'll explore later, external success can be very seductive, even habit forming, but unless we also manage to sustain internal balance and fulfillment, the habit can be dangerous. Few of us prevail with a success-at-any-cost ethic, and of those who do, even fewer genuinely enjoy the consequences.

Negotiating the edge of success is like walking a precipice with expectations of grandeur on one side and fear of failure on the other. To move to more secure ground, you must overcome both illusions and anxieties and develop your *own* philosophy of success — an attainable and personally meaningful one that integrates all aspects of your life. The following chapters will provide guidelines to help you, as well as examples of others who have confronted the edge and moved beyond.

▼

YOUR SUCCESS PROFILE

To determine how your attitudes about success relate to your behavior, complete steps (a) and (b) for each of the following values:

I. Family Values

    a. Rate the following items as
        4 — vital for your personal fulfillment
        3 — very important
        2 — somewhat important
        1 — not at all important

GOAL/VALUE	RATING
Sexual excitement	_____
Marital satisfaction	_____
Having children	_____
Family health and happiness	_____
Satisfaction of parents' expectations	_____
Spending time with your family	_____

    b. Answer the following questions by noting
        A — within the past month
        B — within the past six months
        C — within the past year
        D — more than a year

How long has it been since you
took a day off to spend with your family?	_____
had passionate sex?	_____
discussed your private dreams?	_____
asked for your family's advice?	_____
ate a leisurely dinner with your family?	_____
praised a family member?	_____
taught your child something new?	_____
played a game with your family?	_____
called to chat with an old friend?	_____

▼

YOUR SUCCESS PROFILE

II. Professional Priorities

  a. Rate the following items as
     4 — vital for your personal fulfillment
     3 — very important
     2 — somewhat important
     1 — not at all important

PRIORITY   RATING

Financial wealth   _____
Financial security   _____
Intellectual challenge   _____
Occupational advancement _____
Authority and control over others _____
Personal creativity and expression _____
Attractive work environment _____
Compatible coworkers   _____

  b. Answer the following questions by noting
     A — within the past month
     B — within the past six months
     C — within the past year
     D — more than a year

How long has it been since you
had fun at work?   _____
received praise?   _____
argued with your boss?   _____
received a promotion?   _____
bought yourself a present?   _____
received a raise?   _____
added to your retirement savings?   _____
had an innovative idea?   _____
helped someone else solve a problem?   _____
were fascinated by your work?   _____

▼

YOUR SUCCESS PROFILE

III. Leisure Goals

a. Rate the following items as
   4 — vital for your personal fulfillment
   3 — very important
   2 — somewhat important
   1 — not at all important

GOAL/VALUE   RATING

Physical rest and relaxation   _____
Travel   _____
Physical exercise and fitness   _____
Peace and solitude   _____
Cultural and intellectual stimulation   _____
Political and social activism   _____
Spending time with friends   _____
Creative hobbies   _____
Continuing education   _____

b. Answer the following questions by noting
   A — within the past month
   B — within the past six months
   C — within the past year
   D — more than a year

How long has it been since you
read a novel?   _____
volunteered your time to a cause?   _____
saw, wrote, or called your best friend?   _____
daydreamed without feeling guilty?   _____
researched a topic outside your field?   _____
turned off the phone so you could relax?   _____
went to a play or museum?   _____
enjoyed an hour by yourself?   _____
exercised for more than an hour?   _____
took a vacation without taking work along?   _____

▼

YOUR SUCCESS PROFILE

IV. Personal Goals

a. Rate the following items as
   4 — vital for personal fulfillment
   3 — very important
   2 — somewhat important
   1 — not at all important

GOAL/VALUE   RATING

Emotional and physical well-being   _____
Personal honor and integrity   _____
Social status   _____
Personal independence   _____
Spiritual faith   _____
Personal fame/celebrity   _____
Personal altruism   _____
Friendship/fellowship with others   _____

b. Answer the following questions by noting
   A — within the past month
   B — within the past six months
   C — within the past year
   D — more than a year

How long has it been since you
saw a physician?   _____
prayed?   _____
shared credit for an achievement?   _____
enjoyed seeing your name in the news?   _____
socialized with friends?   _____
gave money to a cause?   _____
enjoyed attending a prestigious social
function?   _____
helped someone less fortunate?   _____
thought about your moral principles?   _____
fought an injustice?   _____

YOUR SUCCESS PROFILE

Now go back over your responses. Do your most recent, or A, activities reflect the values you marked with a 3 or 4? Do most of your D activities correspond to the values you marked with a 1 or 2? If so, your success values and behavior are in agreement. If not, either your values or your activities need adjustment. Reconsider which goals and values truly mean the most to you, and look for ways to activate these priorities in your daily life.

2

▼

M E A S U R I N G
T H E   O B S E S S I O N

To succeed in the world we do everything we can to appear successful.

— *François de la Rochefoucauld*

AMERICA'S CULTURAL obsession with social, economic, and professional status is so pervasive that even if you try to develop an alternative standard for personal success, you may have trouble maintaining it. Just think how many members of the sixties generation who were firmly antiestablishment in their teens and twenties have become vocal middle-aged proponents of upward mobility. Though many maintain their liberal politics and idealism, few are still touting the antimaterialism of the counterculture movement. Having married, started families, and embarked on professional careers, most now appraise their net worth by the same standards they once protested.

Upward mobility itself is not necessarily a curse. Indeed, affluence and recognition are just rewards for dedication, hard work, and productivity. When these are the primary goals, however, they can become relentless taskmasters. When material achievement becomes a driving force, as it is for much of America today, it can throw your life dangerously out of balance. To check the balance, you may need to compare your own attitudes with the yardsticks by which our culture most commonly measures "success": wealth, fame, power, and competition.

The High Price of Wealth

> *Gold is a wonderful thing! Whoever possesses it is lord of all he wants. By means of gold one can even get souls into Paradise.*
>
> — *Christopher Columbus*
> *Letter from Jamaica, 1503*

Columbus wrote these words nearly five centuries ago, but his sentiments are alive and well in modern America. Wealth is still widely regarded as the key to happiness, power, and a kind of immortality. Much more than just a means of exchange for goods and services, money is treated by many as if it really were a ticket to paradise. The dollar has become the predominant measure of success in our society, less because of its purchasing power than its illusory value.

Yet because the illusion changes dramatically in different contexts, wealth is an extremely unreliable standard. The millionaire who appears to be a titan at his public high school reunion may be only a bit player at a New York society ball, and the average couple struggling to keep up their mortgage payments may be tycoons by comparison with a single mother on welfare. Your wealth is defined by the company you keep as much as by the size of your bank account.

The success value of the dollar changes with a person's age as well. Among corporate overachievers, for example, qualification for the fast track depends on earning an annual salary two to three thousand times one's age, and making the fast track, in turn, is supposed to bring increased acclaim, advancement, prestige, and authority. The twenty-five-year-old business school graduate who earns $50,000 his first year on the job considers himself a raving success, but if he's still pulling down the same sum five years later he'll feel like a failure. Inflation and purchasing power are not the real causes of such discontent. Even if prices remain stable and his expenses do not change, the MBA needs a rising salary to reassure his ego that he is progressing. So the price of one's worth spirals constantly upward, making it almost impossible ever to have "enough."

Finally, the importance of money fluctuates with cultural trends. Management consultants and psychologists who have researched the changes in workers' motivation over the past two decades have identified a significant shift toward greater materialism. In the early 1970s, the majority of workers were motivated primarily by the desire for interesting and meaningful work. Career advancement was a secondary motivation, and attaining a high income ranked third in importance. By the early 1980s, however, the lure of an intrinsically rewarding job had dropped somewhat — though it remained the most important objective — and high pay had become the second most important determinant of success. Furthermore, researchers speculate, the materialistic trend is likely to continue, since younger workers seem to be more motivated by money than those of older generations.[1]

Money can buy comfort and facilitate personal freedom, but making money has a way of becoming a habit and seems to prevent the wealthy from availing themselves of true freedom. Distressingly, the lure of money often seems to be directly proportionate to the amount in hand: the more you have, the more you want. The incremental value of each dollar, meanwhile, seems to be *inversely* proportionate to actual wealth: the more you have, the more you need. As Aristotle wrote of people he called wealth getters, "The whole idea of their lives is that they ought either to increase their money, or at any rate not lose it." While Aristotle could not condone the wealth getters, he did not entirely blame them either. "The amount of property which is necessary for a good life is not unlimited," he warned, but "riches and property have no limit."[2] Once you pass into the realm of material wealth, it is easy to lose your bearings.

If you manage to get by on a moderate income, it may be difficult to believe that someone with $2 million could view himself as poor, much less have trouble paying his bills, but among the wealthy this is not at all uncommon. Derek, a real estate developer who came to me complaining of stress, genuinely felt he could not make ends meet on an annual base income of $150,000, even though he had over $2 million in assets. He thought that if I could help him relax and become less anxious, he would be able to earn more, which in turn would free him from the rat race of work and responsibility that was making him miserable. As with most people who are obsessed with money, it never occurred to Derek that increasing his wealth might not bring happiness. He wanted to treat the symptom without acknowledging the disease.

When Derek first appeared in my office he was forty-one but looked considerably older. About fifty pounds overweight, he sagged around his face and middle. Some heavy people appear jolly, but his extra burden simply made Derek seem sad and unkempt. His clothes were obviously expensive, but he wore them carelessly, as if he'd thrown them on in a hurry without checking the mirror. And he had a nervous habit of running his hand through his graying hair as he talked.

"I think maybe I'm losing my grip," he said. "I'm always running so hard, half the time I miss my appointments. And when

I have to make a decision, I feel like somebody's got his fist in my gut and won't let go. In the middle of the night I'll get up and start running projections on the computer just to calm down. I can't sleep. I can't stop. And still I never seem to be getting ahead."

"It sounds like your professional responsibilities are taking quite a toll on your personal life. How is all this affecting your family?" I asked. Derek and his wife had three children, ranging in age from four to eleven.

"There's no real trouble there. I guess I don't spend as much time with the kids as I should, but that's only because I'm working all the time. If I didn't work all the time, I wouldn't be able to pay for the school and the braces and the clothes and the toys and everything else they need. I swear I don't know how anybody manages to both pay for kids *and* spend time with them."

"Do you take any family vacations?"

"Hell no. I can't take the time off. My wife takes the kids places, which is great because I feel less guilty about working late when they're away. But it's been years since I had a whole weekend free, much less a vacation."

"Does your wife pressure you for more money?"

"No. Actually, she thinks I'm a little crazy to be so worried about our finances all the time. But she just doesn't understand about security. If it were up to her, we'd have no savings and we'd end up on the street in our retirement."

To find out how Derek had developed *his* view of security, we had to go back to his upbringing. Unlike many people who become fixated on money, Derek did not grow up in poverty but in affluence. His late father made millions in the timber industry and his mother made her own fortune on stock speculation. For all their wealth, however, Derek's parents had always been extremely tight. They had all the trappings of success — a big house, imported cars, and impressive antiques — but they almost never paid full price. "If I can't get a deal on it, I don't want it," Derek's father used to say, and he meant it. The rule even applied to the household help, who were so poorly paid that they rarely stayed with the family more than a few months. All the money Derek's parents saved went into bank accounts, the interest from which Derek's mother used to multiply her earnings on the stock market. She repeatedly admonished Derek never to touch principal, because that was his security. Derek's father went to his grave without ever touching his principal, and she probably would, too, but it was still vital to have that security.

The message was not lost on Derek. Impatient to start making his own money, he dropped out of college in his sophomore year. At twenty-one he was earning $30,000 a year, but his mother warned him not to become complacent. "You have to stay a little hungry, or else you'll fall behind," she advised him. In response, Derek lifted his expectations while systematically limiting his expenses. He set himself a goal of $5 million and a time limit of twenty years. He found himself a luxury car, but it was used. "When I'm really successful," he explained, "*then* I'll be able to buy a new one." He shopped for nearly two years before finding a house with a bargain basement price in an upscale community. All his neighbors, he was convinced, earned ten times more than he. The more successful he appeared, the hungrier he became.

"Do you still think you would be happy with five million?" I asked him.

"You know," he said, reaching for a well-thumbed memo book in his briefcase, "in today's economic climate and all, that's not really very much money. I've run the numbers and I think that goal was pretty naive." He turned to a page filled with calculations. "In the next ten years alone, what with college for the kids and all this inflation, our expenses are going to top four million. No, it's going to take more like ten or fifteen million to set me free. *Then* I could quit work and really be happy."

Clearly, nothing Derek had achieved amounted to much in

his estimation, yet he truly believed that when he reached his financial goal he'd feel like a king. Money had become a prop for his self-esteem, a substitute for human worth. Until he realized that money alone could *never* make him happy, and until he began to redefine his values and priorities, Derek would continue to teeter on the edge of success, placing his family and his health in jeopardy.

Obsession with wealth manifests itself in a variety of ways, only some of which Derek exhibited. There is a common thread that ties all such cases together, however. At some point, the value of money as a means to Aristotle's good life evaporates, and money becomes an end in itself. When it is placed ahead of love, trust, family, health, and personal well-being, it tends to corrupt. And the more the perceived value of money outstrips its actual market value, the deeper the corruption penetrates. As Saul Bellow wrote in *Humboldt's Gift*, "Hanging on to money is hard. It's like clutching an ice cube. And you can't just make it and then live easy. . . . When you get money you go through a metamorphosis. And you have to contend with terrific powers inside and out." These powers may produce mistrust, envy, and even hatred of anyone who possesses more, and hostility toward anyone who blocks the way to fortune. Sometimes they also generate curious rules about the acquisition or use of money. One person may feel compelled to manipulate or cheat to maximize earnings and then refuse to spend a penny, while another may construct a lifestyle of luxury on a mountain of debt with no hope of ever being able to pay up.

Given the contradictions in society's view of wealth, it is not surprising that we as individuals become confused. Caught between economics and ethics, we strive to maximize our financial solvency — everyone needs a certain amount of financial security and material comfort, after all — while morally condemning those who hoard or plunder great sums of wealth. Ignoring the habit-forming nature of acquisition, we reassure ourselves that we'll magically know when enough is enough and neatly turn off the craving. But not everyone is able to do this. For those who cross over the line, the quest for wealth can become a real barrier to inner fulfillment.

The Quest for Recognition

Ever since Candice and John began going together in college, people had noticed and admired them. She'd been a homecoming queen in high school and was a member of the gymnastics team. He was the journalism department's rising star. His rugged good looks complemented her girl-next-door prettiness, and they believed what their friends told them: that they were the perfect all-American couple.

Shortly after they graduated John and Candice were married, and he was hired as a junior sports reporter by one of the networks. Several years later, when the birth of their child coincided with John's covering the NBA play-offs, his colleagues congratulated him on the air. A few newspapers and magazines picked up on the birth as a human interest story, and in short order the promising young reporter and his family became media darlings.

It wasn't long before John and Candice began competing for the limelight. Even though John was the one whom the network paid to appear on the air, Candice believed that the audience was equally interested in her, the beautiful wife who attracted all the *extra* attention. Without her John was just another sportscaster; with her to boost his image, he could write his own ticket.

Candice's craving for fame could be traced back to the criticism her parents had heaped on her as a child. Her father, a history professor, had never been able to conceal his feeling that she was not very bright. Her mother had tried to steer her toward the fine arts so that Candice could prove that she at least had culture if not brains. But when Candice set her sights on athletics and married a sportscaster, her parents told her she could never possibly amount to anything worthwhile. Candice, determined to make them eat their words, decided that fame would be her revenge.

John, too, was impressed with his own popularity, but he viewed it more as a useful tool on the way to wealth and power than as an end in itself. He would either work his way up to a network anchor position or use his recognition to help him enter politics. Unlike Candice, John could never be satisfied with renown alone. While she was delighted whenever strangers recognized her on the street, John responded only when the strangers were more famous or powerful than he.

As John's career took off, Candice played her role as celebrity wife and mother to the hilt, but it wasn't long before her public, as she'd come to think of them, lost interest. John meanwhile was fast becoming the reigning heartthrob of network news. Soon Candice's resentment of his fame began to push into the open, and the spell he seemed to cast on other women only made matters worse. The marriage was doomed.

Both John and Candice resisted divorce at first because of the negative publicity that was sure to accompany it, but as the rivalry escalated, the prospect of dissolution began to look better and better. Candice in particular longed for the chance to present herself as a savvy, independent woman whose boorish husband had been holding her back. She started scheduling press conferences before the divorce was even final.

For a while the local media covered the divorce and custody battles. A magazine did a profile of the brave and lovely divorcée, and she was invited to appear on a TV talk show to discuss her ordeal and tell what John was really like. Unfortunately, when the subject of John and her divorce was exhausted, Candice didn't have much else to report. Despite her conviction that the public couldn't get enough of her, she had precious little to hold their attention. While John proceeded to move up through the ranks of television journalism, Candice receded quickly into obscurity. Her fall from the spotlight dropped her into a whirlpool of emotions, from rage to jealousy to self-pity, that ultimately left her crushed. Instead of shoring up her ailing self-esteem, her brush with fame finally made Candice feel more inadequate than ever.

While wealth satisfies the desire for status and luxury, fame satisfies the desire for approval and prominence. It makes us feel special. But what constitutes fame varies with the circumstances.

As a college girl, Candice was satisfied with a campus audience, but as her hunger grew, only a national following would suffice. Believing that she possessed a mystique that somehow entitled her to fame, she never felt obligated to do anything exceptional to earn it. As shallow and unrealistic as it may sound, this attitude is quite common among teenagers and young adults who are unusually good looking or charismatic, or who have famous parents. For others the progression of personal fame is more likely to follow a career path, with high school popularity paving the way for widespread recognition within a professional field. A manager might lust after recognition via promotions, awards, appointments to special projects, and interviews in a company or trade publication, but he is not necessarily any less hooked on fame than Candice was; he simply has a narrower audience. Superstars are by no means the only ones who are vulnerable to this preoccupation.

The need to feel special has its roots in early childhood. In healthy, loving families, youngsters receive a quality of affection and attention during their first few years that makes them feel like the center of the universe. At home they *are* superstars, and they naturally come to believe that they are special in the eyes of the world outside as well. While this kind of unconditional love is vital for a young child's self-esteem and security, it also sets a precedent that inevitably is broken with the start of school. In a classroom setting, all children must compete for the spotlight. To recapture the sense of being special, each youngster must discover new ways to win acceptance in school, either by joining the crowd or rising above it.

A certain amount of theatricality comes naturally to children. You may remember mugging for the camera or staging elaborate productions of make-believe plays in your early years. Nothing was as sweet as the applause that filled the elementary school auditorium after each year's class performance. Childhood dramatics, whether on stage, in the classroom, or in the schoolyard, gave you a chance to try on different roles and explore otherwise inaccessible realms, but they also were an acceptable way to win praise and recognition from the adults and the other children in your life. If you happened upon a role that consistently drew applause, you would become famous — at least within your small world — and if you had not yet discovered any other way to anchor your self-esteem, this acclaim would make you feel special again.

The search for a role that will generate recognition continues for many people throughout school and beyond. Some of those who make careers in show business, modeling, or other media-driven industries are motivated by the desire for fame. And many of those who set their sights on the top echelons of business are driven by the same hunger. Somehow, they believe, the acknowledgment and admiration of others will restore a feeling of inner satisfaction that may have been missing since toddlerhood.

In today's world, fame tends to be combined with wealth and prestige as a mark of social superiority, so we naturally expect it to make us *feel* superior. Several generations back, the elite realm of high society was reserved exclusively for bona fide blue bloods. Members of the press were specifically excluded from society gatherings, and the aristocratic grandes dames would take pains to keep their names out of the papers. In recent decades, however, the media have largely taken control of society. Today's grandes dames have their own press agents and assiduously court the social columnists who determine who's hot and who's not. The founding families of modern media — the Luces, Hearsts, and Paleys — are as visible at Manhattan's East Side charity balls as the Vanderbilts and du Ponts, and so are the Reagans, Trumps, and Baryshnikovs of the world, whose claim to social status hinges on power, wealth, and above all, fame.

Fame is not just an entrée into the high life of the here and now but, like the other components of external success, it is perceived as a hedge against mortality. "In contemporary society since the eighteenth century," wrote Erich Fromm, " 'history' and 'the future' have become the substitutes for the Christian heaven: fame, celebrity, even notoriety — anything that seems to guarantee a footnote in the record of history — constitutes a bit of immortality. The craving for fame is not just a secular vanity — it has a religious quality for those who do not believe in the traditional hereafter anymore."[3] But in a culture in which, as Andy Warhol said, everyone will be famous for fifteen minutes, the real power of the spotlight seems to be diminishing. The competition for that footnote in history is so fierce that you could easily spend a lifetime accumulating fame without ever feeling like a bona fide success.

Consider what it takes to be a superstar. To get any real pleasure from celebrity, you must respect and identify with your audience much as you once did with your parents. If you shun or look down on them, they cannot give you the feeling of specialness that is fame's real prize. At the same time, if you want to maintain your prominence you cannot afford to get too close to your audience, or you'll risk getting lost in their midst. By definition, to be famous you must in some way be different and separate from the rest. The inherent contradiction between the desire for acceptance and the condition of isolation can make fame an agonizing obsession.

34

Is it possible to enjoy recognition without becoming hooked? Yes, as long as it is not your primary motivation for achievement. Everyone enjoys being praised for a job well done. The attention and admiration are exhilarating, but also distracting. You can easily get so caught up in playing to your audience that you stop being your own foremost judge and begin to lose the self-sufficiency and character that truly make you special. Then it becomes even more tempting to pursue fame for proof of your worth. Unfortunately, fame is as elusive as it is seductive. The chase may never end.

Wrestling for Power

Power, like fame and wealth, is a relative commodity. Standing alone you may be strong, confident, and independently powerful, but you become powerful in the eyes of the world only when you dominate someone else. Domination may take the form of leadership, authority, influence, or brute force. In any form, though, power is tremendously seductive, for it plays to our natural desire for territorial control. In primitive societies, personal power was gauged by the amount of land and the number of people an individual was able to protect from invasion. Today most of us gauge power by the number of people we can influence emotionally, intellectually, politically, or physically, but the drive for territorial control remains strong. It is what motivates us to seek power, and it is what makes power feel thrilling.

The desire for control may be intensified by conditioning. Certainly our culture prizes power and glorifies those who wield it by promising them a place in history. But an even stronger source of conditioning is the family. If you come from a family that stressed the importance of authority and superiority, particularly if your parents or siblings controlled *you* tightly, then power is probably very important to you. It becomes both a measurement of your worth and a means of wresting control from your family, teachers, and anyone else who may have dominated you in childhood.

Early conditioning can also turn you against power. If your father had a top executive position he did not enjoy, or if your family suffered because of his preoccupation with power, you might make a conscious decision to be less ambitious. Realistically, power involves a great deal of responsibility, uncertainty, and tension, and not everyone wants to assume those burdens.

Still, that subliminal craving persists. You can desire power at the same time that you're terrified of it. And once you have it, you can become obsessed with maintaining it. Whether this happens depends largely on how you obtain power and how you use it. If you are placed in a position of authority because of your talent, knowledge, skill, and experience, and you use your authority to motivate others in positive directions, you may prove yourself a true leader. If you acquire power without demonstrating excellence, however, it can cause your downfall. Managerial ineptitude in business and abuses of power in government are two of the most common, but certainly not the only, examples of the down side of power.

At forty, Alice was hardly a candidate for one of her university's top power-broker positions. A single mother with three teenage children, she held a job as secretary in the sociology department. Neither exceptionally attractive nor bright, she had relied on hard work to squeak through school with a B− average and earn a BA from a small state university. She'd never pursued a profession until divorce forced her to support herself, and this massive university quite intimidated her.

In Alice's department alone, researchers commanded hundreds of thousands of dollars for project grants, and the results of their projects frequently made national headlines. Symposiums on campus attracted world-renowned authorities in every conceivable field, including Nobel Prize winners. The alumni roster was filled with celebrities. But most impressive of all to Alice was the sheer scale of the institution, which sprawled across twenty acres and had a student body of ten thousand, a faculty of several hundred, and a staff of over two thousand.

As she learned her way around and got to know the people in charge, Alice began to feel less like an interloper. Well aware of how few qualifications she possessed, she struggled to appear competent, but still feared that she might be fired at any moment. Her coworkers seemed to like her, though, and no one put her down. Her boss, the head of the department and one of the country's leading experts on terrorism, was particularly generous and encouraging. He often discussed special projects with her and asked her opinion. He also commended her organizational skills, giving her a feeling of accomplishment she'd never known.

Then came the turning point. Alice was preparing the annual report on one of her boss's many research projects when he abruptly asked her how she'd like to run the next meeting of the project committee. As chairman, he usually ran the meetings, but he had to be out of town for the next one, and since she was familiar with the project, he suggested, why shouldn't she take a shot at it? Stunned and terrified of the challenge, Alice nevertheless realized what an important opportunity it was. She nodded mutely, and he handed over the meeting agenda.

As her boss had predicted, Alice managed the committee meeting with aplomb. She kept the focus on the issues, adhered to the timetable, and smoothly organized a vote on the decisions at hand. No one was more surprised than Alice herself. As the others congratulated her on a job well done, Alice beamed in astonishment. She had presided over people who had earned doctorates and advised chief executives, and they were commending *her!* If these people could take her seriously, she must deserve to be taken seriously. For the first time, Alice felt that she had the potential to be more than a secretary.

Alice's boss was pleased with the results of his experiment.

As time passed, he increased Alice's responsibilities and invited her to accompany him to conferences at which he discussed his research with authorities in the field. Because of his work in terrorism, many of these conferences included top brass from the armed forces. Alice felt that she was really making her way up in the world when she began rubbing shoulders with admirals and generals. These men exemplified the way the Real World worked, she thought. They made decisions, won victories, wielded power. They had climbed to the top of the ladder in the military the same way top executives climb their corporate ladders and academics their bureaucratic ones. The system was pretty much the same in every case: to win, it seemed, you had to be a tough, smart, and strategic operator. Alice had never seen these qualities in herself, but to have any chance of success, she believed, she would have to cultivate them.

By the end of her first year at the university, her boss was making sexual overtures to Alice. She was flattered that this brilliant scholar considered her worthy of his affection. Given everything he had done for her, she trusted him. After all, it had been a long time since she'd had a relationship with anyone, and she genuinely liked this man. And if having an affair with him also benefited her career, she thought, what was wrong with that?

Shortly after they began sleeping together, Alice was placed in charge of a small public grant project. Fearful of making the slightest mistake, she surrounded herself with top-notch assistants and learned to work the academic bureaucracy like a delicate machine. Though she occasionally felt like a fraud, she concealed her self-doubts under a mantle of superefficiency. She was a good administrator and her skills deserved to be rewarded, she told herself. According to her observations, all that was missing was some political savvy — the ability to make friends and influence people in high places. If she could develop that ability, she'd have as good a chance of succeeding as anyone else.

In her heart Alice wasn't entirely comfortable with these observations, but what could she do? The system wasn't about to change, and everyone else, particularly her male superiors, seemed to expect a certain level of manipulativeness and deceit. They called it "being aggressive." If she was to advance, it seemed, she had no choice but to accept their standards. Like many other women who find themselves struggling to appear "successful," Alice didn't feel that the circumstances of her life gave her enough clout to challenge the status quo.

Their affair was in its second year when Alice's boss began to seduce a new protégée. Alice was hurt but realized, after a period of soul-searching, that the ending was predictable. This affair was one of her initiation rites. In exchange for a survivable case of heartbreak, she'd received her first career boost. Alice had enough of a track record that she was able to transfer into another department with little difficulty. This time, however, she did not become sexually involved with her superior, and that made her feel even more exhilarated when he handed her a plum assignment: overseeing three interrelated government research grants. She would have to make regular reports in person to the university chancellor and to the grants' godfathers in Congress. As Alice listened to her new job description, she was not deterred by the relatively low pay and the lack of public attention. What mattered was that she would be in charge. How far she had come from her days as a dependent housewife!

Alice managed to climb the bureaucratic ladder for five years before she began to fall. As the scale of her projects increased, outside auditors began to look over her shoulder. They found numerous errors in the financial records, which Alice had never caught, and also noticed that Alice often made exaggerated and undocumented reports on project findings. Despite her apparent flair for administration and her mastery of bureaucratic politics, Alice had never fully developed the scrupulousness her job required. Because her power kept mounting, she felt compelled to inflate her reputation accordingly, even if it meant cheating every now and then. The line had blurred between her own advancement and the job she was expected to perform. Only after she'd been stripped of all responsibility and dismissed from the university without hope of a recommendation even for another secretarial job did Alice recognize just how completely she'd been misled by her own vision of authority.

A powerful role or reputation can assuage internal feelings of weakness and inadequacy. If people perceive you as strong and masterful, you naturally try to bolster those impressions. But the more you submit to external perceptions, the more difficult it is to admit the truth. Alice became so preoccupied with her political standing that she failed to notice when she was no longer doing good work. This tendency of power to bend reality can make it mighty attractive at first, but self-delusion is ultimately dangerous.

One reason is that it is self-perpetuating. When you attain a position of authority, you may find the feeling of control so intoxicating that you keep striving for more. Then your flirtation with power becomes a constant battle to stay on top. The struggle may extend into your personal as well as your professional life and damage or destroy valuable relationships. The executive whose subordinates kowtow to him at work may demand the same level of obedience at home rather than acknowledge his insecurity as a father. The surgeon whose patients view her as their savior may consistently blame her lovers rather than accept responsibility for her dismal love life. In these cases, as with Alice, the trouble begins when *having* power over others is confused with *being* powerful.

The power that we have at any given moment depends on a constellation of factors, the most important of which are other people's perceptions. It's quite possible to secure this kind of power through brute force, threats, bribery, or manipulation. Being powerful requires quite different qualifications. Erich

Fromm wrote, "Being-authority is grounded not only in the individual's competence to fulfill certain social functions, but equally so in the very essence of a personality that has achieved a high degree of growth and integration. Such persons radiate authority."[4]

There is nothing wrong with having authority or enjoying the power that comes with increased responsibility, but the game can turn against you when you begin to view those privileges as your inalienable right. If exercising power seems more important than being powerful, you may be closer to the edge of success — and internal collapse — than you realize.

The Competitive Crush

It is almost impossible to grow and prosper in the modern world without being ambitious. Both internal and external success demand a certain level of drive. But ambition can also generate misery, suffering, and failure.

To understand how ambition can be both useful and destructive, you must first realize that there are two types of ambition: noncompetitive and competitive. One is purely personal and reflects the goals you set for yourself regardless of what anyone around you is doing. The other depends on context and reflects your desire to be recognized or to surpass the achievements of others.

Noncompetitive ambition involves the shaping of your own destiny. It helps you to take control over your own life and get the best out of yourself, as opposed to obtaining power over others. Such ambitions may include the desire to marry, have a family, develop close friendships, achieve a comfortable lifestyle, become expert at certain skills, and explore ideas that personally interest you.

Noncompetitive ambition involves inner passion and direction. It shapes the goals that will ultimately define true success for you. But unless this kind of ambition is balanced, it can also be misleading. Many determined career women, for example, forgo marriage and childbearing for professional advancement without realizing how much their zeal is costing them until, in their late thirties or forties, they suddenly yearn to have children. Single-minded ambition often forces sacrifices that seem inconsequential at the time but eventually cause regret.

Unlike noncompetitive ambition, which is defined by one's internal standards and aspirations, competitive ambition is defined by the actions and opinions of others. The ultimate goal is to dominate others — either directly, by winning authority, or indirectly, by winning recognition as a superior performer. Your competitive ambitions might include your desire to get to the top of your class in school, earn more money than your brother, beat out your colleagues for a plum promotion, or make your division your company's leading contributor to the bottom line.

Most of us require some of both types of ambition, but we tend to focus almost exclusively on the competitive brand, even injecting an element of competition into private goals. Assuming rivalry to be good and natural, we embrace it in education, business, politics, and sports and obligingly endure it among friends, lovers, and family members. Subtly but inevitably, it creeps into decisions regarding where to live, how to dress, where to vacation, and whom to invite to dinner. Unless we make a conscious effort to maintain our private interests, preferences, and goals regardless of how others react, our competitive ambitions can eventually overshadow everything we do.

The predominance of competitive ambition in this country is hardly a new trend. Alexis de Tocqueville noted it when he visited the United States in 1831–1832. Observing the ever-expanding levels of opportunity and mobility in American society, he wrote of an inherent conflict between the competitive quest for success, which he likened to a game of chase with every man for himself, and the nation's need for unity, strength, and excellence. The same observation could be made on a global basis today, as individual businesses and nations fight for control of resources and power while largely ignoring the need for cooperation to resolve the nuclear threat, famine, drought, poverty, and humankind's other urgent crises.

The conflict between competitive ambition and cooperative responsibility is predictable if you consider what it takes to win the competitive edge. You need a certain amount of social detachment to rise above a group, because you may hold back if you identify with others too closely. This basic fact often contradicts the public posturing of competing leaders who pretend to identify with their subordinates (think of a company CEO chatting up the factory workers, or politicians kissing babies and shaking hands with welfare mothers). While it's easy to pretend on the way up that you're responsible to those around you, the inherent isolationism of competition encourages a deeper view of life as a constant battle for control and of outsiders as a persistent threat. The more competitive you are, the more susceptible you are to resentment, mistrust, envy, and hostility toward others.

Ironically, while competitiveness inspires suspicion and criticism of others, it rarely engenders a comparable amount of *self-criticism*. If you set your sights firmly on moving ahead of the pack, you probably will expend far more energy assessing your competitors' positions and measuring the distance between them and you than you will striving for excellence on merit. Particularly in our culture, competition tends to undervalue individual character, discipline, restraint, and virtue while it rewards self-promotion, aggressiveness, and the "killer instinct." Advocates of competition subscribe to a kind of social Darwinism in which survival depends not on humanity or excellence but on domination. This attitude has produced some of the most familiar catchphrases of our times: "It's a dog-eat-dog world," "Only the strong survive," and "It's who you know, not what you know, that counts," to name just a few.

Our culture's emphasis on competition generates an atmosphere in which everyone worries about what's going to happen next while largely ignoring what's happening at the moment. This applies to much of the decision making in government and business as well as to the personal lives of individuals. Being happy and prosperous today is never good enough, because the competition is always gaining, and tomorrow you — or your company or country — might fall out of the lead. The fact that you are constantly looking over your shoulder as you struggle to move forward makes it virtually impossible to attain meaningful goals in the here and now. The present simply does not count.

Competition also encourages you to aspire to superficial goals without questioning their relevance or importance to you personally. One of my patients confessed that she had put in hours of overtime on a project that was not even her responsibility simply to prove that she could do it better than her coworker. Moreover, she had done it at the expense of assignments that she personally felt were more interesting but would receive less attention from the boss. In the end, she did an adequate job on the project and received some recognition for it, but she was criticized for neglecting her own work and her coworker wouldn't speak to her for weeks. Later, when she was assigned a similar project without having to compete for credit, she found it so tedious that she could hardly complete it. Had she concentrated on the tasks that she found inherently challenging and absorbing instead of doing a job simply to show up someone else, she might have discovered a degree of genuinely meaningful success, which in turn might have fueled more far-reaching private career ambitions. As long as she kept taking on jobs that were either beyond or beneath her capabilities, she derived little real satisfaction from her work. Equally distressing, the more she struggled to get ahead, the less she knew what she truly liked or *wanted* to do. Her competitive ambitions had subconsciously barred her from doing work that she found enjoyable and emotionally fulfilling.

Almost everyone has some degree of competitive ambition. In today's world it is virtually impossible to avoid it. But if this drive obscures the goals that really matter to you personally, you will find that fulfillment does not go hand in hand with advancement. Ultimately the satisfaction of surpassing your rivals will wane, yet if you have no deeper passions to fall back on, you may not be able to break your competitive pattern or see the goals that might bring your life into balance.

Resisting the Lures of Success

Of course, wealth, fame, power, and competitive superiority don't appeal equally or simultaneously to everyone. Some people become seduced by one brand of external success, and that leads to the others over time. Other people are so focused that just one of these goals becomes an obsession. Our culture, however, rolls all these temptations into one collective image of success, and therefore we as individuals have to free ourselves from each one before we can establish a deeper personal definition of success.

Challenging the standard assumptions about success does not necessarily mean abandoning them. We all need a certain amount of praise and recognition. We all want to feel that we have some influence over the others in our lives. And we all enjoy the comforts that money can buy. Yet it is quite possible to achieve all these goals and still feel like a failure. They may contribute to our well-being, but they are not essential to a feeling of internal success.

Personal fulfillment arises out of self-respect, pride, conviction, and the love of family and friends. Aristotle's deceptively simple statement that happiness is the result of "living well and doing well"[5] illustrates just how vague and personal a notion fulfillment is. Until you figure out just what "doing well" means to you, your ambitions are liable to fluctuate aimlessly with your circumstances. You may view success as health when you're ill, wealth when you're in debt, power when you're feeling downtrodden — in short, whatever you happen to be lacking at the moment. Achievement then becomes a means of filling a void, of patching over your inadequacies, of covering up your failings. Instead of capitalizing on your assets and moving to new heights — instead of truly doing well — you allow your shortcomings to dictate your up side. Success and frustration become inextricably linked.

When we talk about having it all, we really mean living well and doing well: having the outer rewards of external success and the personal fulfillment of internal success. Attaining either of these goals is not easy, and sustaining a balance between the two can be even more difficult. To make this balancing act work, you need to have a firm grasp of your own ideals as well as a keen understanding of the terms of success imposed on you by others. The standards of your profession, the social expectations within your community, and the values of your family and friends are all bound to influence your expectations for yourself, but you need to know where the outside pressure ends and where your internal passions begin. To find this dividing line, you may have to go all the way back to childhood, which is where the next chapter will take you.

46

▼

CONFRONT YOUR OWN OBSESSIONS

What roles do money, fame, power, and ambition play in your life? To find out, choose one response to complete each of the following statements.

I.

1. If I had $10,000 to play with, I'd use it to
   _____ a. invest in the stock market.
   _____ b. take a well-earned vacation.
   _____ c. buy something I really need.

2. I would rather have
   _____ a. a designer ring worth $3,000.
   _____ b. a more beautiful ring designed by a friend, worth $2,000.
   _____ c. my great-grandmother's wedding ring worth $1,000.

3. When buying a car, I look for
   _____ a. high resale value.
   _____ b. attractive design.
   _____ c. comfort and mechanical reliability.

4. If forced to take a pay cut or leave a job I love, I would
   _____ a. look for a higher paying, even if less fulfilling, job elsewhere.
   _____ b. look for a similar job with comparable wages elsewhere.
   _____ c. stay and reduce my living expenses.

5. No matter how much money I have, I never seem to
   _____ a. have enough.
   _____ b. worry about it much.
   _____ c. have trouble making ends meet.

II.

6. If I worked in broadcasting, I would be a(n)
   _____ a. anchor.
   _____ b. producer.
   _____ c. technician.

7. If asked to model for a national fashion magazine, I would
   _____ a. leap at the chance.
   _____ b. do it if the pay was satisfactory.
   _____ c. refuse.

8. When my name is in the paper, I
   _____ a. clip the article and show it to my friends.
   _____ b. read the article and mention it to my family.
   _____ c. don't tell anyone.

9. I think TV commercials are most persuasive when they
   _____ a. feature a celebrity.
   _____ b. feature a professional expert.
   _____ c. don't use a spokesperson.

10. When I attend a live performance and the emcee asks for audience participants, I
    _____ a. sit right up front.
    _____ b. sit where I can best see the performance.
    _____ c. hide in the back.

III.

11. I would rather be
    _____ a. a boss/employer.
    _____ b. my own boss.
    _____ c. a supervisee/employee.

12. When someone questions my authority, I
    _____ a. feel defensive.
    _____ b. try to analyze the situation objectively.
    _____ c. ignore the challenge.

CONFRONT YOUR OWN OBSESSIONS

13. I
    _____ a. need to control everything that happens to me.
    _____ b. like to be in control of certain situations.
    _____ c. keep myself open to impulse and surprise.

14. People gain power in society by
    _____ a. attaining high standards of excellence.
    _____ b. working well within the system.
    _____ c. manipulating and deceiving others.

15. Having power over others makes me feel
    _____ a. excited.
    _____ b. responsible.
    _____ c. anxious.

IV.

16. To advance in my career, it is most important for me to
    _____ a. prove that I'm better than the competition.
    _____ b. prove that I can get the best out of others.
    _____ c. get the best out of myself.

17. I do my best work when
    _____ a. I work independently.
    _____ b. I work with a partner.
    _____ c. I work with a team.

18. I would most like to
    _____ a. have a high public profile with lots of admirers.
    _____ b. be known and respected within my occupational field.
    _____ c. have the respect and loyalty of a few close friends.

19. When I beat someone out of a promotion or award, I feel
    _____ a. proud.
    _____ b. pleased but chagrined.
    _____ c. too guilty to enjoy it.

▼

CONFRONT YOUR OWN OBSESSIONS

20. I like to win
    _____ a. at all costs, in everything I do.
    _____ b. and will cheat if the opposition is cheating.
    _____ c. when I deserve to win, as long as I've played
       fairly.

Evaluation

The following table will help you interpret your responses.
Count the number of (a), (b), and (c) responses, and enter the
total for each section in the appropriate column.

		TOTAL NUMBER		
Questions	*Measure*	*a*	*b*	*c*
1–5	Money	_____	_____	_____
6–10	Fame	_____	_____	_____
11–15	Power	_____	_____	_____
16–20	Competitive ambition	_____	_____	_____

Groups in which you have three or more (a) responses point
up your success obsessions. Groups in which you have three
or more (b) responses indicate success criteria that are mod-
erately important to you. Groups in which you have three or
more (c) responses designate the success trappings that are
least important to you.

PART II

THE PUSH TO
BE SOMEBODY

3

▼

LEARNING TO STRIVE

"I always wanted to be the teacher's pet. If I got the best grade in class or was picked for some special job, I felt like I was on top of the world. If the teacher ignored me or picked someone else, I felt like a total reject. And because I was always competing with the other kids, I never felt real comfortable socially."

— *Kyle, age 17*

"I wanted my son to succeed at everything he did. I couldn't stand to see him fail or show weakness, so I tried to shelter him from situations that were too difficult. I guess I was afraid that if he didn't succeed, it would mean that I had failed."

— *Anne, age 49, Kyle's mother*

THINK BACK to your earliest childhood memories. Remember playing by yourself for hours? Remember the elaborate games and stories you wove into make-believe, the intensity with which you drew pictures, built Tinkertoy palaces, and learned to pitch and catch? Were these early pastimes work or fun — or both? If you consider your youthful activities "mere child's play," take another look.

53

Consider the passion, the skill, the talent, and the perseverance that went into those first explorations. Think of all you
learned about art, literature, science, and drama. Finally, consider how proud and pleased you felt over even minor accomplishments. The activity itself and the sense of discovery were
your primary rewards when you were very young, and that's
the critical difference between child's play and the work of school
and adulthood. Only as you grew up did you begin to absorb
the message that accomplishments must bring some kind of praise
or reward to be worthwhile.

Accepting this message meant losing two of the essential keys
to inner fulfillment: the ability to respond to your own curiosity
and creativity and to embrace a challenge just for the fun of it,
and correspondingly, the ability to find pleasure and challenge
even while doing tasks that might otherwise seem boring. You
can rebuild these capacities and retrieve the sense of wonder
and enthusiasm that came so naturally in your early years. To
do so, however, you may need a brief refresher course on what
it's like to be a child.

The Nature of a Child

We love to romanticize early childhood as a kind of grace period
free of pressures and demands, a time of growth and development but not much real accomplishment. Nothing could be further from the truth! From birth, infants face a huge and essentially alien world, the rules of which they must quickly learn in
order to survive. In addition to language, manners, and social
customs, these rules encompass far more complex issues, such
as the limits of personal identity and authority, the distinction
between make-believe and reality, and the gap between desire
and gratification. An American tourist arriving in an aborigi-

nal settlement in New Guinea would be in more familiar territory than a newborn struggling to make sense of family and society.

Yet the baby learns the fine points of this world far more thoroughly and quickly than any grown tourist in a distant land. In part this is due to genetic predisposition, which, like an internal map, guides the child's physical, intellectual, and emotional development. But an even more important part of the formula is the baby's natural enthusiasm for learning. You don't have to pressure or bribe an infant to walk or talk, even though each of these milestones requires an extraordinary amount of effort, practice, and determination. Likewise, if you observe a normal, healthy three-year-old over the course of a day, you probably will marvel at his nonstop outpouring of industry, experimentation, and inventiveness. In the guise of play and with no ulterior motive but fun, youngsters routinely test the laws of physics, experiment with language and the arts, dabble in botany and zoology, hone their athletic skills, and learn the rudiments of mathematics. They truly are Renaissance explorers, fascinated by all the intricacies of life and society.

Children naturally tap into sources of creativity and curiosity that seem to be closed to many adults. The more they draw on these internal wellsprings, the more satisfaction they get from their play. This is why youngsters generally tend to be more enthusiastic about drawing on blank paper than in a coloring book or paint-by-numbers set. Originality is inherently more satisfying than conformity, yet the prevalence of such programmed devices indicates how we steadily pressure children to prize conformity over their natural instincts and impulses.

It's important to distinguish between discipline and conformity. We all need to be disciplined enough to survive within the general rules of society, respecting the boundaries between ourselves and others while upholding our rights as individuals. Discipline is about setting and observing our own limits so that

55

we can lead safe, productive, fulfilling lives. It is about initiative, perseverance, and faith rather than blind compliance. Discipline fosters creativity; conformity deadens it.

Many of our cultural traditions demand conformity under the pretense of discipline. Religious sects, preparatory schools, ethnic, regional, and professional subcultures, all have codes of behavior, dress, and values to which participants must adhere, whether or not these codes are articulated. In these worlds, true personal discipline may resemble nonconformity, and so bring rejection.

Thanks to this common misrepresentation of discipline, parents often have difficulty deciding where discipline ends and conformity begins. Many equate acceptable behavior with perfect imitation. Very early in life, children may start to get the message that it is wrong to try a different approach or vary from what's expected. That is how the sources of creativity and curiosity become blocked and stagnation sets in. From this point on, external rewards begin to supplant intrinsic motivation.

Rejuvenating the creative forces that run so strong in early life is a vital step toward personal fulfillment, whatever your profession or goals. Whether you are an executive, mathematician, scientist, or homemaker, creativity will help you to embrace and develop new ideas and to try different approaches to solve problems. The more flexible and open you are to a variety of options, the more opportunities will reveal themselves, and the more satisfaction your efforts are bound to bring.

According to Teresa Amabile of Brandeis University, an expert on creativity, there are three essential requirements for creative accomplishment, two of which are either present or available from the earliest years of life. The first consists of the raw material: inherent ability or talent, basic information, and natural curiosity. The more varied an individual's interests and abilities, the more creativity is likely to flourish. The second necessity is practiced skill: concentration, diligence, familiarity with existing ideas and techniques, the ability to apply various methods and use appropriate instruments or tools. This is the one area of creativity in which extrinsic motivations can be useful, because so much of practice involves repetition and tedium that is not inherently rewarding. The third and probably most important element of creativity, which is so abundant in childhood and often lacking in adulthood, is the sheer delight of exploring and experimenting for their own sakes.

The first and last of these requirements for creativity are ready to be tapped almost from birth. If raw talent and enthusiasm are cultivated and later strengthened through practice and technical proficiency, intrinsic motivation can develop naturally. Unfortunately, many parents focus right from the start on the skills and inadvertently squelch much of their children's natural talent and enthusiasm for experimentation. Instead of encouraging natural interests and enthusiasms and providing opportunities to learn through play, these parents are most concerned with neatness, obedience, adherence to schedules, and academic accomplishment. Infants are trained to recognize letters on flash cards. Toddlers receive lessons in test taking. Grade-schoolers are signed up for violin, ballet, and tennis lessons before they can ride a bike. Too often youngsters are told what to believe, how to behave, what to learn, and how to look. If they fail to measure up, they must absorb the pain of disapproval and sometimes rejection.

Competitive ambition underscores this kind of parental master planning. Consciously or unconsciously, almost all parents want their offspring to be somehow better than the rest, and most measure superiority not in terms of individual expression but by comparative performance. The push to excel occurs even during pregnancy as mothers-to-be earnestly compare the activity and size of their babies in utero, but competition begins in earnest at birth, with comparisons of birthweight and length, Apgar scores, alertness, and sociability. Speed is the ultimate criterion of superiority as parents watch to see whether their child will crawl, walk, and talk ahead of the rest.

Parent and Child

Parental attitudes about success and competition would be largely irrelevant if it weren't for the intense bond between parent and child. The infant's natural dependency gives parents vast influence over this fledgling person, and this influence in turn breeds parental possessiveness. If you are a parent, you know how easy it is to view your baby as an extension of yourself. You take personal pride in his or her achievements and feel guilty or frustrated over each failing, however minor. Your progeny, after all, can enhance your personal image and possibly compensate for some of your mistakes in life. Early on, your child learns to distinguish victory from defeat on the basis of your reactions. Your cheers express triumph, your winces or frowns, defeat. One of the great challenges of parenthood is to balance closeness and separation, pulling back far enough that your child can pursue his or her own interests without feeling compelled to please you, but not so far that the bond between you is broken.

From the child's point of view, this bond is a source of great comfort and security early in life, but it generates increasing conflict later on. Because of the close identification, the baby automatically imitates the parent without distinguishing negative traits or tendencies that undercut the child's natural instincts and talents. Eventually, however, the joint identity is bound to unravel, for no matter how much a parent may want to control or live through a child, differences in temperament, personality, ability, and interests are bound to arise. For a child to emerge healthy from the attachment and separation process, parents need to encourage a balance of intimacy and autonomy from the very beginning.

You can see the results of this process by the time a child enters school. Of course, personality, temperament, gender, and other individual factors all have a tremendous influence on any child, but the behavioral differences in the following cases can be traced primarily to the boys' relationships with their parents, especially their mothers. All three of these four-year-olds came from families with two working parents and no siblings, but the similarities end there.

Even though Kyle's mother left him with a sitter for several hours each day while she went to an office, he was never out of her grip emotionally. In theory, she let him do whatever he wanted, yet she pounced on him whenever he took the slightest risks in play, and she hovered warily nearby whenever he was around other children or adults. Not even her husband was to be fully trusted, since he spent far less time with the boy than she and was, she felt, too strict and not attentive enough. Not surprisingly, Kyle was fearful and suspicious of anyone outside his family and extremely possessive of his belongings — just as his mother was possessive of him.

By the time Kyle was two years old he had begun to express his need for a separate identity in the only way he knew: by having tantrums. Reserving his tirades almost exclusively for his mother, Kyle hit and bit her, screamed, and flailed his arms whenever he couldn't have his way. Horrified by his behavior, she was nevertheless terrified that he might reject her if she tried to discipline him. She couldn't bear to test Kyle's love, because deep down, she lacked the confidence to trust him or herself. So she pulled him ever closer and tried to baby him just when he most desperately needed her to step back and give him firm, mature guidance. Instead of learning the rudiments of self-respect and discipline, Kyle emerged from each tantrum feeling as frustrated and confused as his mother.

His problems intensified when he started going to preschool three mornings a week. While most of the other mothers stayed at school with their children only for the first few days, Kyle's mother rearranged her work schedule so she could stay "as long as he needed" her. Sensing her reluctance to let him go, Kyle obligingly cried for his mother to stay with him every day. But as long as she was there, he felt entitled to special treatment from everyone else as well. When he could not be the center of attention in class, he withdrew and insisted she play with him. This went on for almost eight months until, at her husband's and the teacher's insistence, Kyle's mother finally agreed to leave him at school.

Despite his initial screams and sobs of protest, Kyle adjusted to her absence within days, but his social patterns remained largely unchanged. He routinely grabbed toys from others but threw a full tantrum if anyone dared touch an object in his possession. He was incapable of initiating play with another child, yet when he was ignored he sulked or sought relief from the teacher, whom he viewed as his best friend. In Kyle's mind, the game of school was to compete with other children for the teacher's approval, and whenever she praised him or smiled at him, he beamed with the pleasure of success. Kyle had been so well trained to depend on his mother's approval that in her absence, he transferred his need for acceptance to the next available authority figure. To curry the teacher's favor, he finally developed more socially acceptable behavior, but he was not really at ease or happy among his peers or on his own. This pattern promised to persist through his school years and later into his work life — the boss would become his higher authority and motivational source.

Brian's view of nursery school was altogether different from Kyle's and, not surprisingly, so was his home life. For starters, Brian's parents agreed about most aspects of child rearing and openly discussed areas of uncertainty. Brian's father had taken an active role in his son's life from infancy and helped with everything from diaper changes to trips to the park. The young woman who cared for Brian during his parents' workday was enthusiastic and affectionate toward the little boy, and she conferred with his parents about even minor issues or problems so that consistency was maintained.

Brian's parents weren't afraid of losing their son's love, and they felt strongly that by learning to respect others, Brian would also learn to respect himself. Consequently they weren't afraid to say no to him when he overstepped reasonable limits, and they absolutely refused to tolerate any abusive or disrespectful behavior from him. Brian was encouraged to take on challenging projects that would exercise his imagination and to take pride in his accomplishments, whether they involved singing an impromptu song, scribbling a picture, or building a sand castle. He was also taught early on to clean up after himself, to say please and thank you, and to share his possessions with a minimum of complaint. Whenever Brian acted out, he was given the choice of either calming down immediately or being isolated until he felt better. Because this treatment was so consistent, Brian quickly learned that there were more peaceful ways to get what he needed, and he also discovered that he could survive without always being the winner.

By the time Brian began school, he had a firm foundation of self-esteem that allowed him to roll through conflicts with relative ease. He could be happy playing by himself or with other children, being a leader or a follower, holding the teacher's attention or listening to her praise another child. Freed from the kinds of power struggles that dominated Kyle's daily life, Brian was able to focus on tasks of play and discovery. He could immerse himself for long stretches in games of make-believe, painting, climbing the jungle gym, or building sand castles. As he progressed through elementary and upper school, Brian would have to endure competitive pressure from teachers and peers, but at least in his early life he was able to develop his unique capacity for joy and creativity. He would be able to draw from these reserves for the rest of his life.

If Kyle stormed through early childhood and Brian swam, then Dominic drifted. When the teacher asked for volunteers, Dominic tried to hide. While the other children played together, Dominic amused himself in a corner. When the class was supposed to be working on an art project, Dominic doodled and daydreamed. Undemanding and a little goofy, he seemed lost in a fantasy world most of the time.

Dominic had constructed his fantasy world long before he entered school. It was his defense against a family that generally ignored his existence. Both his parents were driven professionals who worked long hours and had little attention to spare for their son. They assigned his care to a housekeeper who spoke almost no English, and they rarely questioned her decisions on his behalf. The housekeeper, unfortunately, viewed her job as primarily custodial and did not even try to compensate for the lack of parental affection. Most of the time Dominic was left to his own devices in a large house with lots of expensive toys, and he did the only thing he could: he retreated into himself.

Dominic's parents wanted a model son to show off as another symbol of their success, but Dominic was just an ordinary kid. No one looked twice at him on the street. He was quiet and withdrawn around strangers, and he didn't have any obvious talents or qualities that his parents could boast about. Since no one was willing to make the effort to draw him out or build his self-esteem, the little boy quickly slipped into the shadows of family life.

In school Dominic was overwhelmed by the level of activity, stimulation, and competition. The teacher tried to befriend him, but with ten other children to supervise, there was only so much she could do. When she expressed her concern in conference to Dominic's parents, they defensively insisted there was nothing wrong with their child and insinuated that the problem lay with the teacher. Although she suspected the cause of Dominic's withdrawn behavior, the teacher knew she would only make trouble for herself by interfering, so she essentially gave up. Dominic was left to wander distractedly through his days, neither competing with nor relating to the other people in his life. Without more determined intervention from another teacher or outsider later on, Dominic would remain adrift for the rest of his childhood. At some point, he might fasten onto some protected and creative career, or he might strive to become materially successful in an attempt to finally capture his parents' approval. But he might also simply drop out. In any case, until he resolved the emotional alienation of his early life, the joy and self-trust so necessary for internal success would not come easily.

In all families, parents are primary role models with tremendous influence over their offspring, but how each child eventually assimilates that influence is largely determined by the quality of attachment. Ironically, parental values and beliefs tend to dominate children most in families like Kyle's and Dominic's, in which the emotional attachment is either very tight or very tenuous. When the parents are highly competitive and demanding, the children feel they have only two choices. They can adopt the same attitudes and try to secure parental approval by becoming externally successful, or they can reject these values entirely as a means of punishing their parents. Children who grow up with a comfortable sense of attachment as well as confidence in their own individuality tend to develop a more objective view of life. They may select some of the same goals as their parents, but these choices generally are determined more by personal preference than by emotional angst.

Attitudes about success are a core part of the parental legacy. They are, in fact, reflected in almost all the values parents hand down, so youngsters learn from a very early age what constitutes success within the family belief system. Consider your own upbringing. If your parents placed a high value on material wealth and status, you may have gotten the message that form counts more than substance; what schools you attended, what grades you brought home, and what clothes you wore may have received more attention than the quality of your friendships or the nature of your dreams. If your parents struggled so hard to make ends meet that they never seemed to stop and enjoy life, you may have inferred that relaxation and pleasure are unworthy indulgences, that you should feel guilty for enjoying yourself. If your parents sacrificed their own needs so that you could receive an education and "get ahead," you may feel obligated to accept their vision of success even if your personal ambitions are more modest.

In many families success means surpassing parental achievement according to parental standards: making more money, winning more professional recognition, earning a more impressive title, or achieving greater fame. All too few children are taught to equate success with personal fulfillment and happiness, and those who develop this definition for themselves are often admonished by their parents.

I was discussing this issue with a group of marriage counselors when one woman confessed that her son was a furniture maker in a small town in the Pacific Northwest. "He does absolutely beautiful work," she said, "and he tells me he's never been happier, but I have such difficulty accepting that after college and graduate school and all the opportunities we've given him . . . he's really nothing but a carpenter!" This woman wasn't proud of her feelings and she sincerely wished she could develop a different attitude, but she was being honest. Given her own values, she could not view her son's chosen life as a success. Fortunately, however, she had worked hard to achieve a good balance of attachment and autonomy in her relationship with her son, so he was able to pursue his own goals without feeling guilty or wrong, and mother and son still had a close relationship despite their differences. In many other families in which the parent-child relationships are not well balanced, the child may spend a lifetime trying to please, surpass, or provoke a parent, either by following the approved route or by rebelling and choosing a lifestyle intentionally designed to insult the parent.

Few parents consider that external success, which seems so appealing, can be harmful. Most assume that if they provide love, their children naturally will be happy. But they also believe that unless children are pressured to compete, they may forfeit happiness to failure. Consequently parents often begin grooming their youngsters to be overachievers at an early age. Through lessons, classes, educational toys, and highly programmed schedules, the children are supposed to develop discipline and cultivate the special skills needed to get into the top schools, get the top grades, receive the most awards and attention. In theory this sounds fine: the more information and the more learning opportunities a young child is exposed to, the better equipped he or she should be for a successful life. However, this approach rarely produces the desired results.

For one thing, when a highly demanding and programmed schedule is imposed on a youngster, there's little opportunity for that child to become *self*-disciplined, organized, and motivated. Instead of becoming a self-starter, the student is taught to depend on parents and teachers for inspiration and encouragement.

Another serious problem is that the message of love can be drowned out by parental concerns over a child's competitive performance. Psychologist Paul Bracke conducted an experiment with sixth-graders and their parents in which the children, blindfolded and with one arm tied behind the back, were instructed to stack blocks for eight minutes while parents watched from the sidelines. The parents who were most aggressive and impatient coached their youngsters with an average of twenty-five comments or suggestions per minute. "That these parents were so invested in their children's performance on a meaningless task perhaps gives an indication of the pressures some kids in this country face," remarked Bracke.[1]

"I'm giving you all these opportunities because I love you and want the best for you," the parent may insist, but often what the youngster hears is "I won't love you or care about you unless you prove that you're better than other kids."

For all their good intentions, parents often cultivate extrinsic motivation in children at the expense of intrinsic motivation. They play up the importance of external approval by using praise, prizes, and special benefits as a not-so-subtle form of bribery. Frequently a child is offered a reward from the parents in exchange for a reward from the world outside: a dollar for every A at school, a special dessert for every badge at Scouts, a new toy for every ribbon at swim meets. Pretty soon the youngster is so busy working for prizes that there's little time, energy, or inclination left for idle curiosity or personal interests that do *not* command a gold star.

The focus becomes increasingly narrow, with achievements such as neatness, imitation, speed, and control receiving more attention than ideas or originality. Instead of being encouraged to discover the inner satisfaction of working at a task or learning new information for its own sake, the child is trained to perform only as instructed. If no reward is forthcoming, there's no reason to work. The very powerful reinforcement effect of external rewards undercuts the more subtle motivation to take pride in a job well done. When bribery is used routinely it tends to destroy the personal inspiration and passion from which true fulfillment arises.

This is not to say that rewards are altogether useless or damaging. On the contrary, the promise of an extrinsic reward can sometimes give you the incentive to accept challenges and opportunities that you might otherwise pass up, and thereby introduce you to new sources of intrinsic fulfillment. A friend persuades you to run a mile with him, for example, by offering to buy you dinner, and as a result you discover that jogging makes you feel good. After that, you won't need an external incentive to keep running. As long as you don't become dependent on the secondary prize, there's no harm done.

When your primary motivation is intrinsic, praise and recognition can add tremendously to the satisfaction of doing something well. Financial compensation not only adds to job satisfaction, but in adulthood it gives you the practical security you need to concentrate on work you enjoy. However, when your main reason for doing a job is to get the reward, your performance and your sense of fulfillment are apt to suffer. Working for love produces far better results than working for money, and bonuses are more gratifying than bribes.

Many parents argue that they are merely preparing their children for the real world, which measures success in prizes. It's true that much of our culture in general and the business culture in particular emphasize extrinsic motivation. Risk taking, complexity, personal exploration, and inquisitiveness are widely discouraged. Manners, dress, presentation, and subordination are largely stressed over substance. The focus is on a narrow bottom-line and short-term gain with a steady climb in productivity. Anyone who backslides, even in an attempt to boost productivity in the long term, may be subject to punishment. Despite the recent explosion of publicity and literature about quality and excellence being revalued in the business community, the prevailing corporate attitude continues to reward quantity over quality and conformity over creativity. But if you've been conditioned from childhood to submit to these priorities, are you really any more content to live with them in adulthood? Probably not.

However, if you were encouraged as a child to develop that

initial sense of delight and to pursue your personal interests and goals without worrying about success or failure, you may be less vulnerable to the reward systems of later life. You are more likely to view your work as a form of play, creating ways to challenge yourself as you go rather than focusing tightly on the money or praise you will get when you finish. If you were able to develop a wide range of interests and skills in early life, you may feel less confined by your job or other immediate constraints. Having a reservoir of personal talents and dreams can save you from feeling that you are defined solely by the roles you play for others. It can give you the perception of freedom that allows you to rise above superficial limits. Without this deeper insight into yourself, you might easily feel trapped when circumstances seem to move beyond your immediate control or when you can no longer meet other people's expectations.

Unfortunately, parents are not the only ones who have mistaken assumptions about competition and external success. Many similar notions predominate in our educational system. As a result, the rules of achievement that you learned at school may have intensified your dependence on extrinsic motivation. In the next chapter you'll discover how competition in the classroom, dovetailed with parental influence, can perpetuate the myths of external success.

▼

CREATE A HISTORY OF YOUR
SUCCESS CONDITIONING

To discover how your deepest attitudes about success were formed, look as far back into your childhood as you can remember and, on a separate sheet of paper, jot down your answers to the following questions.

1. When was the first time you can recall receiving your parents' approval?
2. When was the first time you can recall receiving your parents' disapproval?
3. What did your parents want you to be when you grew up?
4. What did *you* want to be when you grew up?
5. What did your parents do for a living?
6. Did your family have strong traditions and values that you were expected to uphold? If so, what were they?
7. Did your parents schedule your activities, or did they teach you to organize your own time?
8. Did your family encourage you to express yourself artistically? If so, did they urge you to develop your own style or to imitate the style of famous artists?
9. Did your parents encourage you to be like others your age, or did they encourage you to resist peer pressure?
10. Did you feel you had to earn your parents' love and approval?
11. When did your parents reward you, and what did they offer as rewards?
12. What rewards gave you the greatest satisfaction?
13. Did you feel you deserved the rewards you received? Did you feel you often deserved to be rewarded when you were not?
14. What were your favorite toys, and what can you remember about them?
15. What did you like to do in your free time? Note how your favorite activities changed from early childhood into high school.

▼

CREATE A HISTORY OF YOUR
SUCCESS CONDITIONING

16. What were your favorite subjects in school, and why?
17. Did you enjoy school more at one point in your childhood than another? If so, when did the change take place, and why?
18. Were you given the encouragement and opportunity to pursue the subjects and activities that most interested you?
19. Did you worry about your report card? Why?
20. As a teenager, did you worry about getting into college and getting a job when you grew up? Where did that pressure come from?

Through your responses you can see how your attitudes toward achievement and success developed during early childhood. Keep this personal history handy and refer to it as you read the following chapters; it may yield some insights into your later performance and career choices.

TRAINING FOR THE COMPETITION

It is the contest that delights us, not the victory.
— *Blaise Pascal*

RUSSIAN-BORN pianist Leopold Godowski and violinist Mischa Elman were in the audience when Jascha Heifetz made his American debut at Carnegie Hall. Listening to the sixteen-year-old violinist play, Elman began to sweat and squirm in his seat. "Isn't it hot in here," he whispered to Godowski. "Not if you're a pianist," Godowski answered slyly.[1]

This anecdote demonstrates just how powerful the competitive drive can be, throwing the body out of whack and distorting our most basic perceptions, without our even realizing what's going on. For many of us, competition is like a sixth sense, keeping us always on the alert for rivals who might move ahead of us on our chosen path to success. Taking it as a given that only a few can reach the top of any one field, we struggle to absorb the tricks and talents of those already up there, but are often distracted by those who appear to be advancing from below.

Between these two conflicting preoccupations, it's easy to lose sight of our own accomplishments.

How does this obsession get such a hold on us, and how can we shake ourselves free to concentrate on our own lives instead of everyone else's? To answer these questions, we have to retrace our basic training in competition, which, for most of us, began in school.

The Social Maelstrom

Just as parental attitudes about competition and attachment can affect our perceptions of autonomy, creativity, and success, the way we interact with the outer world is determined largely by our social and academic experiences at school. The combination of parents and schooling shapes our values and sense of identity in fundamental ways.

A child just starting school begins a social and emotional transition that will continue through high school to college and beyond. The object of this transition is to find a comfortable place in the crowd, which may seem a simple goal on the face of it. But young children are inexperienced in dealing with crowds of any sort, so school demands some very big ego adjustments. Children who have been spoiled at home must learn to share the stage with their classmates. Children who have been neglected at home must learn to stand up for themselves and to trust the people around them. Youngsters who have received discipline and love and have had prior experience in group situations may make the smoothest adjustment to school initially, but they still must learn to cope with the endless social permutations that occur throughout childhood. The lessons are never easy.

Before completing this transition, most youngsters go through some or all of the following phases:

1. Feeling adrift or isolated within the crowd
2. Needing to feel like the star or leader among their peers
3. Becoming followers, determined to "fit in" by imitating their chosen group in dress, language, and behavior
4. Carving a comfortable niche within the crowd by establishing an independent, but not alienated, sense of individuality

Looking back to your own school days, you can probably remember how you handled these different stages. Think about your first impressions of kindergarten: a roomful of strangers; an unfamiliar adult who would tell you what to do and what not to do; a whole new set of rules and routines to follow; a world without your mom or dad in which you were on your own. Most children experience feelings of isolation and anxiety during the first few days of school, but not everyone proceeds through the stages of socialization in the same way. These patterns are affected by each child's personality and temperament, relationships at home, and the social dynamics within the school setting.

Some children take years to move past those original feelings of alienation and withdrawal. They may become the class wallflowers, mortified when their peers or teachers single them out for attention — even praise. Their greatest desire is simply to get through school without being noticed, and they may dream of adulthood as a kind of fantasy world in which they will finally find understanding and acceptance.

Youngsters whose alienation stems from low self-esteem and who receive little emotional support at home have great difficulty developing the internal strength and social skills necessary to achieve true fulfillment in later life. The clumsy boy whose parents babied him and who grew up in the shadow of popular older siblings, had trouble making friends, and, instead of dating, worked in the audiovisual department through high school, is not magically going to bloom with self-confidence when he reaches college. Instead, he may find a career path that promises continuing obscurity, like computer programming or accounting. His notion of success may be to maintain a secure income and a low-key lifestyle, and to get married. He won't actively choose to shun competition; he will flee from it out of insecurity and fear.

Another youngster may remain socially withdrawn or become alienated later in school as a result of a specific traumatic incident or series of incidents. Educational psychologist Kaoru Yamamoto researched the power of peer disapproval by presenting children with a hypothetical choice between undergoing surgery and wetting in front of classmates. The knife was unanimously preferred over the humiliation of peer ridicule.[2] Given this intensity of peer pressure, not even a parent's wisdom or soothing words are likely to comfort the girl who bumbles hopelessly through every gym class or the boy who becomes the class bully's favorite whipping boy. From this kind of humiliation, the child may develop a perceived self within that particular school setting that he or she feels powerless to change. Instead of competing socially, such youngsters often pour their energy into schoolwork, competing academically and achieving unobtrusive excellence. Alternatively, if they receive strong family support and have the necessary social skills to start fresh, they may be able to overcome their negative image through camp, religious activities, or other group activities outside school. If all else fails, such youngsters usually leave their perceived self behind when they change schools, graduate, or move on to college. Once their reputation dissolves, they can afford to take emotional risks and resume the socialization process, moving through the same phases they otherwise would have faced up to much earlier.

The third pattern that occurs with youngsters who feel alienated from their peers is characterized by a preoccupation with
revenge. These youths don't turn to their schoolwork just as a
diversion or comfort but as a defensive maneuver to get back at
their more popular classmates. You drive yourself to become the
best athlete (usually in a non–team sport like track or swimming), artist, student, or musician, and thereby prove your superiority over those who have snubbed you. Then they will feel
like failures, and you will be the hero. The problem with this
"I'll show them" attitude is that it never really heals the wounds.
Even if you eventually become the most sought-after student on
campus or, later in life, the most respected professional in your
field, you will always suspect that you are popular for what you
have done rather than who you are. Deep down, the hurt child
is still there, and you are apt to remain emotionally isolated and
mistrustful. Only when you are able to embrace that child and
stop evaluating yourself solely through the eyes of others can
you start to believe in your own success.

If at any time you were known as the class leader, comic, bully,
prankster, or actor, you know just how compelling the spotlight
can be. On the one hand, the attention of teachers and peers is
a substitute for parental attention. On the other, it creates the
illusion of importance within the school culture and compen-
sates for feelings of inferiority and isolation. The kid who has a
public reputation as a clown can tell himself that everybody knows
and likes him, that because he is special, he no longer has to
worry about being lost in the crowd. The trouble is that his comfort depends on his reputation, and audiences can be fickle and
cruel. Unless the class clown can keep coming up with fresh and
funny jokes year after year, the laughs of admiration may turn
to derisive snickers. Most youngsters who try this route to acceptance eventually discover that it doesn't produce the results
they truly want. Those who continue to believe in the sparkle of

the spotlight can become obsessed by the desire to stand out in later life, as Kristin was.

My first impression of Kristin was just what she wanted it to be. In her mid-twenties and stunning, with waist-length blond hair and a tawny California tan, she had perfected the kind of entrance that was guaranteed to make people take notice. Her stylish wardrobe and the effortless way she moved across the room radiated the poise and self-confidence that she'd been conditioned to display from childhood.

Kristin was the only child of upper-middle-class parents who had always encouraged her to be the best in everything she did. Her mother, who told her she was the most beautiful girl in the world, filled her daughter's closets with clothes of just the right color and cut to enhance her features. When Kristin got older, her mother taught her how to use makeup, how to select flattering clothes, how to arrange her hair, how to walk, sit, and stand gracefully. She also warned Kristin to watch her diet and clucked over every slip or indulgence.

Kristin's father, meanwhile, insisted that it was not enough for her to be pretty; she had to prove her superiority in other areas as well. He coached her in her studies, taught her to play the piano, and arranged for her to take lessons in horseback riding, Latin, and ballet.

Kristin fully believed she was as special as her parents wanted her to be and was determined to prove it. She worked hard, made good grades, and in high school became class president and captain of the cheerleading squad. With glowing recommendations from her teachers and parents' friends, she got into an Ivy League college and left home fully convinced that she was destined for success.

Moved onto a new stage, however, Kristin found it much more difficult to recapture the spotlight. Academically and socially, the competition was stiffer than she'd ever imagined it could be.

The stress involved in just keeping up was tremendous, and she responded to it by overeating, which quickly led to bulimia. She'd been conditioned never to allow herself to become fat or average, and now that both suddenly seemed real possibilities, she was desperate. However, she found it as difficult to recreate her star status as it was to maintain her figure in this competitive environment. Instead of stellar grades, she got B's and C's, which plunged her into depression and made it even more difficult to keep up with her studies. She began to miss deadlines and skip classes. Kristin knew she had the ability to get by, but that just wasn't good enough. If she couldn't stand out, she wouldn't even try. After a year and a half, she flunked out, for the first time distinguishing herself through failure rather than success.

Crushed by this defeat, Kristin retreated into marriage to a self-effacing real estate broker who made her feel special once again. Her husband was noncompetitive, nonthreatening, and told her she was wonderful. He pumped up her ego and repeated what her parents had always said: that she was a born star.

"I have a sparkle that sets me apart from other people," she told me during one of our early sessions. "I have a great contribution to make." But she had no idea what that contribution would be. She was employed as a waitress and enrolled in a community college, and was considering a career in communications. In this profession, she thought, her looks would give her a natural advantage.

At the same time, Kristin was retreating from her marriage. The man who had put her back up on her pedestal was beginning to bore her. He did not have a sparkling personality or an exciting career, and despite his supportiveness, she felt he was actually holding her back.

"People must wonder what I'm doing with someone so average," Kristin said, dredging up the dreaded specter she'd been fighting since childhood. "I think I'd be a lot happier with some-

one who's more widely admired and respected. It would challenge me to establish my career more quickly, and surely I would
feel more successful being with someone I considered successful!"

Kristin had been so conditioned to identify herself with her
image that she had never learned to get her own bearings, set
her own goals, or judge her own actions without thinking first
of her audience. Now the lack of direction was catching up with
her: her need for recognition was holding her hostage.

There's a hidden undercurrent of tension, uncertainty, and suspicion among some school-age youngsters. Beneath the surface
playfulness and innocence of youth, a kind of social maelstrom
simultaneously engulfs children and distances them from one
another. You may remember from your own childhood how un-
predictably people could change. One day you and your best
friend were inseparable, and the next your friend was courting
someone else. For years the boy who sat next to you hardly spoke
a word, and then in junior high school he ran for class president!
And what about the girl who was homecoming princess one
year, and by the next had become so withdrawn that none of
her old friends could talk to her? Everyone juggled similar emotional and physical changes, but in many different ways. This
created an oddly conflicted social atmosphere of camaraderie and
mistrust. You wanted to lean on your friends, to confide your
deepest hopes and secrets, but were never sure you could really
depend on them.

Within that turbulent atmosphere, groups provided a feeling
of safety and comfort. Particularly during early adolescence, when
the social dilemmas were compounded by active separation from
parents and the chaotic physical and emotional changes of pu-
berty, the desire to fit in became intense. After the age of ten or
eleven, kids tended to travel in packs, and it was sometimes
difficult for a casual observer to tell one member of the pack

from another, as each had the same wardrobe, mannerisms, hair style, lingo, activities, and interests. Identification with a group was a means of denying personal changes that seemed just too hard to accept.

As a transitional phase, such group identification can provide a positive sense of belonging and self-esteem. One danger, however, is that it can also quash individuality; in struggling to fit a uniform mold, you rejected your uniqueness and empowered the group to define you. By accepting the external view of success as popularity, you may also have compromised your values and self-reliance. As long as you were accepted by the group, you felt okay about yourself, but what if you slipped out of grace? *That* was something that happened only to losers, and as long as you identified yourself by the company you kept, you didn't want to take any chances. For fear of rejection, you tried to conform. The pressure to conform made it increasingly difficult to trust your internal judgment and to develop individual instincts and goals.

The more exclusive a group is, the more desirable it seems; you may be attracted to an "elite" club without knowing anything about it except that it is difficult to gain admittance. By the same token, though acceptance into a selective group is usually a passive feat, it creates the illusion of accomplishment. It is not surprising then that youngsters, divided between the desire to be adopted by a group and the need to feel special, are drawn to cliques.

Restrictive groups encourage the same kind of caste and class distinctions that in adult society are based on race, money, prestige, fame, power, and family name. In high school the criteria for membership might include looks, social grace, humor, toughness, political activity, and athletic or artistic talent. Those rejected from one club often form "I'll show you" groups, creating a spiraling progression as each contingent struggles for peer acceptance. Yet the very triumph of acceptance into one coterie can mean exclusion from all others. Once the lines are drawn, anyone crossing them must pay a heavy penalty. Nowhere are these divisions better illustrated than among today's urban youth gangs, who maintain exclusivity by deadly force.

The danger in such groups, be they street gangs or varsity clubs, is that they can engender a false sense of belonging. You believe in the veneer of camaraderie and understanding that knits the group together and feel protected by it. Sometimes the fabric is tight enough that genuine friendships develop, but just as often the unity is superficial. When the group disbands or you no longer qualify for inclusion, you may be abruptly abandoned.

If you are able to sustain the desired social standing through school, you may gravitate toward similar groups in adulthood. But adult cliques, too, can be cruel, as Tom Wolfe aptly illustrated in *The Bonfire of the Vanities*. When a streak of bad luck and questionable choices dented his upper-crust veneer, Wolfe's antihero received neither sympathy nor support from his equally upper-crust friends, associates, or even family members. Instead, the ranks closed against him, and he realized for the first time how tenuous social success can be.

You may have discovered the limitations of group culture while still in school. Perhaps differences developed between group members, making it difficult to maintain a unified front, or maybe you just grew tired of the pressure to conform. Having achieved separation from your parents, you may have felt more confident about facing life on your own terms without clinging to your peers for reassurance. At this point, you were ready to apply your individual talents and new self-assurance to your personal goals without feeling an urgent need either to stand out or to imitate the rest of the crowd.

Healthy youngsters move through some or all of the intermediary phases en route to the final stage of comfortable individuation. Others, however, may get stuck between phases, particularly during high school and college. Failure to make it in the "in crowd" can follow one through life, sometimes breeding bitter defiance. The Ivy Leaguer who strives for success so that his former classmates will be forced to admit "Gee, he isn't the wonk we thought — his Pulitzer Prize proves it!" is still caught between the desire to be one of the guys and the compulsion to prove how special he is. This kind of ongoing desire for social acceptance can turn into a drive for more and more external badges, but these achievements, in and of themselves, rarely bring complete satisfaction.

Terms of Achievement

School, mirroring society at large, relies on external recognition as a primary motivator and all too rarely gives children the tools they need to judge their own performance. Instead, the terms of achievement are defined by others. Grades and academic awards are determined by teachers. Popularity, club membership, and class offices are designated by classmates. Constant emphasis on what others will think discourages the view of learning and accomplishment as a source of internal satisfaction and tends to crush individual interests and talents that are out of the mainstream.

In school you are taught to view excellence as a comparative measurement rather than a personal one. University of Chicago researcher Benjamin S. Bloom describes how this process works: "The instructor expects a third of his pupils to learn well what is taught, a third to learn less well, and a third to fail or just 'get by.' These expectations are transmitted to the pupils through school grading policies and practices and through the methods and materials of instruction. Students quickly learn to act in accordance with them, and the final sorting through the grading process approximates the teacher's original expectations."[3] When teachers grade on a curve, they do not assess each student's performance individually. The students who are failed one year may do as well as the students who receive C's the next, or as well as A students in another school. Having achieved the same objective level of performance, one group can be stigmatized as failures while others are hailed as academic champions.

Compound the teachers' comparisons with those incessant peer comparisons, and the notion of personal excellence, or mastery, diminishes even further. Remember how you and your friends compared report cards? Earning an A meant that you'd succeeded only if your best friend got an A − or less. And if you did the best job you could and learned a tremendous amount, but the teacher awarded you a C and your buddy a B, that grade immediately negated your sense of accomplishment and made you feel like a loser.

The reliance on external standards encourages competition for external approval and, consequently, can create a ceiling on achievement. If you were very bright and could easily outperform the others in your class, you probably had little incentive to work harder; why bother striving to be the best you *could* be when nothing in the system challenged you? If you lagged behind the others academically, the effect may have been even more negative; why bother struggling when you were told you could never catch up? Bloom's research proves conclusively that "failure (or inadequacy) in a school subject effectively closes it for further consideration."[4] At both ends of the academic spectrum, the tradition of defining excellence as a comparative measurement tends to undermine individual initiative.

In 1968 Bloom introduced an alternative educational model based not on comparative ranking but on personal accomplishment. Mastery learning, as the concept is called, assumes that all students can master a given task if given the appropriate materials, instruction, and time, and if they are evaluated by objective rather than comparative criteria. A flexible teaching plan is key, since students learn at different rates and require different amounts of instruction and reinforcement.

In general, three-fourths of students taught under mastery conditions achieve the same level of performance as the top one-fourth of students in traditional education.[5] Furthermore, because the mastery system emphasizes the use of small group study units and eliminates comparison grading, it minimizes classroom competitiveness. And because it increases the likelihood of academic excellence for every student, it tends to enhance students' self-esteem.[6]

As promising as these findings are for the students in mastery learning projects, they sound an ominous note for the rest of us, past and present students of traditional educational systems. Not only has our competitive orientation cost society the skill of low achievers who might have excelled under different learning conditions, but it has largely undermined our capacity for teamwork and trust. In the classrooms of our youth, students were rarely allowed to pool knowledge on tests or work together on research projects. Such prohibitions, coupled with comparative grading policies, conditioned us to view one another as opponents.

The adversarial undertones in the classroom aggravated already shaky social bonds, heightening maliciousness and mistrust between individuals and between groups. In academic and social contexts, divide and conquer was a legitimate path to victory. Knocking out the competition often seemed easier than demanding more of yourself, especially if you'd never been encouraged to discover your personal best. Hence, a standard competitive strategy was to undermine everyone else and win by default. Remember how this worked? If you didn't feel like studying or couldn't grasp the information to be covered in a test, you would downplay the test's importance, wrest a few friends away from their books to come play, make fun of friends who were studying diligently, or create a distraction that would destroy their concentration. As long as your buddies weren't acing an exam, you felt it was okay to blow it yourself. It wasn't how much you'd learned that mattered but how you compared with your peers.

Competitiveness can exact a heavy emotional toll. It distorts the value of work and achievement and tends to encourage competitive drive, energy, and tension, often at the expense of genuine talent, skill, and personal welfare. The more ambitious you appear, the more promising others will think you are, regardless of your actual merit. But surpassing others and doing well personally are often conflicting goals. Competitive ambition usually is fueled by fear of failure, and fear of failure can create deep anxiety. In one recent year alone, three apparently unrelated suicides occurred among students in a public high school in an affluent area of southern California. Of these, one was triggered by the student's failure to make the tennis team and one by failure to make the debate team.

Behind the competitiveness we absorbed in school is an assumption that if you fail to win, you're a loser. Indeed, within the black and white of the academic world, there is constant tension between winning and losing, passing and failing, being accepted and being rejected. This zero-sum, or winner-take-all, thinking does not end with school, and it poses a significant threat to our political and economic systems. The standard extremist view that one system of government should prevail points to annihilation in the nuclear age, while the corresponding economic view of trade as a contest for supremacy points to the monopolization of industry and the demise of the middle class. Zero-sum thinking pushes each side to the wall and forces otherwise unthinkable reactions.

The Three Faces of Competition

Fortunately, the competitive model that we were taught in school is not entirely representative of the world at large. Despite the tendency of certain governments, corporations, and individuals to view competition as a struggle for conquest, the vast majority accept it either as the price of maintaining a job and a lifestyle or as a useful incentive to take on new and potentially rewarding challenges. While it is almost impossible to survive in this culture without some competitive drive, the challenge is to master the three faces of competition so that your ambition serves you without damaging your life. This crucial issue is rarely addressed in the classroom.

Offensive competition is characterized by the drive to get to the top, to beat out everyone else, to dominate the field. This is the form of competition that arises naturally out of the zero-sum values we're taught in school and that most people associate with success in the business world. Erich Fromm described it as a "psychological premise of the industrial age."

> It means: that I want everything for myself; that possessing, not sharing, gives me pleasure; that I must become greedy because if my aim is having, I *am* more the more I *have*; that I must feel antagonistic toward all others: my customers whom I want to deceive, my competitors whom I want to destroy, my workers whom I want to exploit. I can never be satisfied because there is no end to my wishes; I must be envious of those who have more and afraid of those who have less. But I have to repress all these feelings in order to represent myself (to others as well as to myself) as the smiling, rational, sincere, kind human being everybody pretends to be.[7]

While offensive competition often encompasses goals such as wealth, fame, and power, the main attraction is the sheer thrill of surpassing others. Although this sensation tends to fade quickly, it is so potent that it can preempt normal safety mechanisms such as judgment and objectivity and create an ongoing hunger for victory. Offensive competition, after all, cost investment banker Ivan Boesky a $100 million penalty for insider trading, the equivalent of his 1985 income. It brought down the executives of the Wedtech Corporation who resorted to bribery, theft, and forgery to beat out the competition for lucrative Defense Department contracts. And Canadian track champion Ben Johnson lost his gold medal when it was discovered that he had used steroids in his effort to beat Carl Lewis in the 1988 Seoul Olympics.

The notion that offensive competition is necessary for achievement is largely a myth, according to researchers. Psychologist Robert Helmreich of the University of Texas headed a team that studied the relationship between competition and success among students, scientists, academic psychologists, airline pilots, airline reservation agents, and business people. Seven different studies conducted during the early 1980s produced the same results: in every group, the individuals who were most determined to outperform their colleagues ended up with the lowest levels of achievement, as measured by grades, salaries, professional citations, and promotions. These findings match those of studies focusing on journalists, employment agency interviewers, and other professional groups, as well as more than one hundred studies focusing on student performance.

Competition per se is not the culprit, since those who performed best in these studies tended to have a strong drive to excel. It was the nature of the competitiveness that made the difference. Those who were mistrustful, secretive, manipulative, and more concerned with winning than performing or enjoying their work had the lowest achievement levels.

These findings are supported by investigations of recent air crashes, which pin much of the blame for these disasters squarely on the macho competitiveness among cockpit crews. After investigating a rash of near misses and accidents at Delta Airlines in 1987, the Federal Aviation Administration concluded that flight crews were "frequently acting as individuals rather than as members of smoothly functioning teams."[8] In 1978 a United Airlines plane ran out of fuel near the Portland, Oregon, airport, crashing and leaving ten dead, after the captain repeatedly ignored warnings from the other officers that the fuel levels were low. And in 1982 an Air Florida plane crashed into the 14th Street Bridge in Washington, D.C., and plunged into the Potomac River, leaving seventy-eight dead, despite the copilot's having warned the captain four times that conditions were too dangerous for a takeoff. The problem is so widespread that many airlines have instituted a training program called Cockpit Resource Management, which teaches flight officers cooperative skills.

Not only can offensive competition hold you back at work, it is potentially harmful personally as well. The urgent need to win can drive a wedge into your marriage, turning what ought to be a trusting, equal partnership into a contest for power and personal validation. If you have children, your competitiveness may cause you to pressure them to perform when young, but you may feel threatened when they later begin to assert their independence and demonstrate talents that rival your own. Even in recreation, the constant push to prove your superiority can make you so compulsive about athletic performance and fitness that you increase your risk of injury and deprive yourself of the emotional benefits of exercise.

Because the focus is always on the future and the sole objective is to keep winning, this type of competition generates high levels of anxiety and discontent. As one of my patients who is married to a compulsively competitive clothing salesman described it, "This week he got a phenomenal order and he's high as a kite. Next week his orders will drop back to normal and he'll be in a massive depression. He spends his whole life on edge." The roller coaster effect is almost unavoidable if you become hooked on winning, and this can endanger your physical, mental, and emotional health as well as your personal relationships.

When I point out these dangers to my most competitive patients, they usually try to put me off by saying that everything will change once they finally make it to the top. Like Derek's prediction that he would feel successful when he had a net worth of $5 million, it's an illusion. Once you're in the grip of greed and fear, enough is never enough. Even if you always win, you may find it impossible to accept yourself as a success, because there's always the chance that you might lose tomorrow, and then you'd be a failure. Fortunately, there are other ways to play the game.

Defensive competition involves protective rather than aggressive gamesmanship. Most of us are defensive competitors by nature — that sixth sense is working all the time. We want a comfortable life, with our share of material advantages and economic opportunities. We want our efforts and accomplishments to be duly acknowledged. We do *not* want anyone to threaten our loved ones, physical possessions, or personal or professional reputation. Yet wishing alone doesn't bring the desired results. We have to support our desires with action, determination, and a certain amount of strategy.

The object of defensive competition is to secure what is rightfully yours — to maintain those aspects of life you most care about — as opposed to striving for the top. In a utopian world where everyone respected one another's rights and where the resources were shared equally by all, this type of competition might evaporate. In a world that is full of offensive competition and relatively short on economic justice, however, defensive competition is necessary for survival.

On the positive side, this brand of competition keeps us on our toes, makes us look alert, prevents us from stagnating. It pushes us to strive for excellence so that we are less vulnerable to attack from the outside. It encourages us to monitor and learn from our competitors, thus broadening and strengthening ourselves. And because the ultimate goal *is* survival, it discourages the bravado and manipulativeness that are endemic to offensive competition.

On the negative side, defensive competition can degenerate into jealousy and envy when we feel our achievements are being threatened or surpassed. Such emotions can produce mistrust and greed, the same impulses that often weaken offensive competitors.

Incentive competition serves as a short-term impetus to push yourself to a high level of personal mastery or accomplishment. It is the challenge that makes you try activities or investigate ideas that you otherwise might resist. It is the friendly office rivalry that sees you and your colleague through a mandatory project that neither of you really wants to do. It is the competition that exists for no other reason than moving you forward and introducing you to new opportunities for fulfillment. Incentive competition tends to lose its motivational effect relatively quickly. It does not keep you interested in pursuits that do not prove intrinsically fulfilling, but it is very useful as an introductory push or a tactic to help get you through a particularly difficult task.

Incentive competition is most effective in relatively simple tasks that require no outside assistance. If you and your colleague are instructed to address and seal one hundred envelopes each, racing may motivate you to work more efficiently. If your assignment is to write a customized computer program, however, your performance will benefit more by your concentrating on the job, and possibly teaming up with your coworker, than by your competing. David and Roger Johnson, who have reviewed more than 120 studies on competition and cooperation, warn against relying on competition:

Currently there is no task on which cooperative efforts are *less* effective than are competitive or individualistic efforts, and on most tasks (and especially the more important learning tasks such as concept attainment, verbal problem solving, categorization, spatial problem solving, retention and memory, motor, guessing-judging-predicting) cooperative efforts are more effective in promoting achievement.[9]

Whether a particular contest or assignment involves offensive, defensive, or incentive competition depends largely on the attitude you bring to it. While you may view your Sunday tennis match as an opportunity to improve your stroke, another player may see it as a battle for court supremacy, and still another might consider it a means of maintaining social or athletic standing. Your view of the competition does not necessarily determine whether you will enjoy the game, but it directly affects the amount of stress you feel while playing and how you react to the score.

Place yourself in each of the following situations to see how you respond to the different faces of competition.

1. You haven't played tennis since junior high school, the semester you flunked gym. Now your neighbor has invited you to a game on her new court. You balk. "Oh, come on," she cajoles. "If you lose, I'll buy you dinner as a consolation prize. If you win, you buy me dinner to celebrate!" You accept the challenge, only to discover that your game has actually worsened over the years — and your friend makes good on the consolation prize. Are you glad, or sorry that you played?

2. You are attending a sales conference at an upscale resort, and tennis is de rigueur for all the executives. On the court, you face off against a broad range of skill levels, from that of your boss, who usually loses, to that of your associate, who used to be a tennis pro. While you are playing, your mind is on the presentation you're scheduled to make that night. You lose the game with your associate, but beat your boss. Do you wish you'd pushed harder to win both games?

3. Your brother-in-law is aggressively competitive in everything he does, and when he challenges you to a tennis match, you know that he's determined to see you lose. You're quite a good player, however, so you agree to the contest. But, you warn, you have to leave within two hours to pick up your daughter at school. Two hours later, you are still playing ferociously, and the score is tied. Do you end the game and go to get your daughter, or do you persist in trying to win?

As you can see, it's not the situations but the participants who are competitive. You can strive to be the best in your field — whether that means being the best parent, professional, or manager — without also striving to pull the rug out from under everyone around you. You can work to maintain and gradually improve your reputation and still be supportive of others who share similar goals. You can take advantage of your own natural feelings of competitiveness to help you through difficult or tedious tasks and to lure you into potentially rewarding new interests. Be aware, however, that the more importance you place on winning, the more tense and anxious you will probably feel. Your state of mind, in turn, may warp your performance and actually cause you to lose both the internal and the external success games.

The Cooperative Advantage

What makes competitiveness in our culture so dangerous is not competition itself but the assumption that competition and cooperation are antithetical. In fact, the better you are able to cooperate and utilize cooperative strategies, the more successful, or competitive, you are likely to be. The clearest evidence of this can be found in those rare innovative businesses that apply cooperative management techniques.

▼ Coworkers share resources and information.

▼ Positive interdependence reigns: coworkers depend on and help one another to succeed, instead of trying to undermine one another. Mutual trust and encouragement are emphasized.

▼ Each person has a unique role and is accountable to the group.

▼ Coworkers within each group share credit: no one person steals the glory.

▼ Teamwork is defined as the combined efforts of individuals, and each member is encouraged to demonstrate and teach the others any special skills or concepts he or she develops. This prevents individuals from either becoming submerged in the group identity or hoarding their own discoveries. It is the business equivalent of team spirit in sports.

In a cooperative business, each group might be assigned a single project. The group members then divide the work among themselves. They use peer review to keep one another on track, and they present their final results collectively. The group, not the individual, receives credit, but each person's job performance is evaluated individually, with cooperation being considered an important part of performance.

Researchers have found that workers in cooperative settings tend to be more attentive and to complain less than workers under traditional management. Both individual and group productivity receive higher qualitative marks, and quantitative production usually is higher as well. Particularly when projects involve complex issues and intricate tasks, the cooperative approach seems to produce better results. Interestingly, the benefits begin to fade as soon as competition is introduced, even if it involves team competition. An atmosphere of full cooperation, among as well as within company teams or departments, seems to produce the best results.

The benefits of cooperation spill over into participants' social interaction, tending to decrease prejudice engendered by ethnic, racial, or handicap differences while improving relations between workers and management. Participants in cooperative programs tend to be more engaged in their work, report greater satisfaction and interest in their jobs, and have more confidence in their capabilities and skills.

Blending a cooperative approach with your own positive competitiveness can bring gratifying results, but it is difficult to do on your own. Your life is not a controlled office setting or factory floor where everyone can be instructed to abide by cooperative ground rules. If you are surrounded by power-hungry associates at work and status-conscious family members at home, you may not be able to persuade them to change their attitudes. However, you don't have to let them dictate yours.

The first step is to reduce your reliance on offensive competition as much as possible. You don't have to fight to prove yourself. In fact, the more desperately you want to win, the less faith you probably have in your ability to do so. If you believe in yourself, you feel less pressure to prove yourself in the eyes of others, and you are more likely to excel.

The second step is to accept that you need other people to help you get ahead and feel successful. You don't live in a vacuum, and you can't achieve fulfillment in isolation. The delicate balance between accepting yourself as an individual and defining a place for yourself within society is the culmination of a socialization process that began when you first set foot in school. If you cannot achieve this balance, you may end up either losing yourself in the rat race or segregating yourself in your quest for external success. Interweaving healthy competition with cooperation can help you achieve the desired balance.

The third step is to open yourself to the free flow of ideas and skills that constitutes cooperation. If you are driven by competitive ambition, you may stubbornly resist other people's suggestions, or you may take them at will but refuse to share your ideas for fear of losing credit. If you accept cooperation as a success tactic, however, you have the benefit of others' information and feedback. Contrary to zero-sum theory, not every contest need produce losers. By availing yourself of the cooperative advantage, you can succeed at your chosen goal *and* assist those around you to succeed in theirs.

After Brooke's first few sessions, I knew that she was extremely competitive. She, however, felt that her expectations and behavior were all part and parcel of achieving success as a working woman. By striving to win, she was doing what she had to do — what she'd always been instructed to do. She was divorced, alienated from her family, and had too little time for her four-year-old son, but although these problems were making her miserable, she couldn't understand why they were afflicting her or what she could do to resolve them.

Brooke had not sought treatment of her own accord. Afraid that her erratic pulse rate indicated heart trouble, she'd consulted her internist, who determined that she was not having heart problems but panic attacks. He referred her for therapy, which she was convinced she did not need. She was, after all, a stylish, bright career woman who at age twenty-nine earned upward of $65,000 a year as a buyer for a major department store. She was a winner, not a loser, and in her mind psychological counseling was for losers.

Given her resistance, we approached her problems obliquely, starting with the past instead of the present. I asked when she had first recognized her ambition to have a successful career.

"Why, as far back as I can remember!" she answered without hesitation. She sounded genuinely surprised by the question, as if it had never occurred to her that children might grow up without craving success. "My parents were very big on competition, especially my father. I have a sister and two brothers, and Dad turned everything we did into a contest. We'd get stars for doing our chores, and extra stars for doing them on time or volunteering to do more than our share. It was always a contest to see who had the most stars. My parents also compared our grades and gave a special treat to the one who had the best report card. Every weekend we'd play touch football on the front lawn, and Dad would be pretty hard on any of us who didn't want to play or didn't play to win. He was a salesman with a big electronics manufacturer, and he used to lecture us that only winners get to the top, that we had to be winners at everything we did."

"It sounds as if you've followed his advice. Does he think you're a success?" I asked.

"He sees my career pretty much as I do," Brooke replied, shrugging. "It's middling. I'm on track, but I'm not there yet."

"How will you know when you *are* there?"

A look of confusion passed across her face. "Why, when I reach the top of the ladder," she replied, as if it was so obvious that she'd never given it much thought. "When I no longer have to compete with anybody."

"So your goal is to be able to stop competing, and the only way to achieve your goal is to compete," I said, trying to clarify what she'd told me by rephrasing it.

"Put that way it sounds sort of stupid, but yes, I guess that's about right," she answered with a short laugh.

"Are your brothers and sister as competitive as you are?"

"We had the same upbringing," she said curtly. "They're doing their own things, and I guess they're all pretty successful. We keep tabs on each other through my mother, but I don't talk to them."

"What caused the falling out?"

"There's too much manipulation when we're together. Little digs. Games of one-upmanship. It's as if we all feel we have to outdo each other, as if we're still fighting for those gold stars."

"Sounds as though you don't enjoy being competitive."

Brooke bristled at the thought. "Competition is a reality, a fact of life. I enjoy winning, and if you're going to win you have to compete. But with my family no one ever really wins, 'cause no one ever concedes defeat. Finally, I just decided to pull out of that game."

"What if they declared you the winner?" I asked. "What if you achieved such professional success that none of them could even come close. Would you want to see them then?"

Her face saddened as she struggled with her reply. "I'm sure, whether I admit it or not, part of the reason I'm so ambitious is to compete with them. So yes, I suppose I'd feel like showing off if I became that successful. But I don't honestly know if winning is the solution. They'd probably just resent me more. We'd still fight and mistrust each other. I'd like our family to be close, but I'm not sure we know how to do that."

In another session we focused on Brooke's divorce. She'd been married to an aspiring actor whom she'd met in school. They'd begun as equals, but with ambitions that led in different directions. Brooke's produced a steady climb, with promotions and salary raises every year or two. Even in her outside activities she always rose to the top, becoming president of their homeowners' association and chairing the fund-raising committee for the local Red Cross. Her husband, Jack, meanwhile, performed a string of bit parts in small-theater productions and supplemented his income by driving a cab. When they decided to have a child, he volunteered to stay home so that Brooke could return to work after just three weeks of maternity leave. During the following three years Jack virtually stopped working and let Brooke support them. He insisted that he'd pick up his career again once their son began school, but Brooke no longer believed that he would ever be a success. In her own home she was a winner without a contest. She couldn't respect Jack because he had chosen not to compete. In her view, they would never again be equals.

But now that they had broken up, Brooke realized with concern, she was overwhelmed by her role as a full-time parent. The panic attacks had started just after she obtained custody of her son.

"Did you consider compromising, letting Jack have custody or sharing custody?" I inquired.

"No, I couldn't do that. I may not have as much time for my son as I would like, but I love him with all my heart. It would kill me to have our contact reduced to visitations. Besides, on my salary I can provide for him far better than Jack ever could."

"How is your son handling the situation?"

She gulped, her eyes filling with unbidden tears. "He fights all the time. He tells me he likes Jack better, that he wishes he lived with Jack." Then she sat up straight and brushed away the tears. "I'm sure this is a natural part of the transition. He's going through the biggest change of all of us. We'll get there . . . but it is *so* hard!"

Brooke remained in therapy for nearly a year, during which time she moved into position for a big promotion that, while good for her career, did not excite her personally at all. Here was yet another move that she felt compelled to make solely for the sake of winning. If she refused it, she argued, her boss and coworkers would think she'd lost her competitive edge. Her mother would worry that she was losing her senses. Her siblings would gloat. Her father would reject her. The only person whose opinion did not seem to matter was Brooke herself.

As we proceeded to peel away the layers of conditioning that had made Brooke so competitive, I encouraged her to pick out the pieces of her past that had given her the most pleasure, regardless of whether they contributed to her eventual success. At first she had difficulty even thinking in such terms. It was as if ambition had smothered her memory of joy. I hoped it had not also crushed her capacity for happiness.

Gradually, though, the weight lifted and she began to accept her right to enjoy life outside the battle zone. She reached back in time and extracted memories of her brothers and sisters as friends instead of combatants. She remembered how much she'd enjoyed art in school until her father had examined some of her creations and pronounced her untalented. She recalled the fun she'd had one summer during her adolescence working as a camp counselor. The job hadn't paid much, and even then she'd worried that it wasn't much of a career starter, but the camp was by a beautiful lake and the kids were good-natured and liked her, and she'd had a genuinely good time. The only time she'd ever felt as relaxed and happy since then was when she and Jack and the baby took a two-week vacation in Hawaii.

"Funny," she commented. "I fought tooth and nail to avoid taking a vacation so far away. I was afraid I'd miss something really important at the office if I was out of touch. But Jack insisted, and as soon as we got off the plane, I remember, I could actually feel the pressures fall away from me. I was surprised how good it felt to be free."

"What happened when you returned from that trip?"

"Oh, I stepped right back into the grind. Then things started to deteriorate between Jack and me, and we never took another vacation like that."

"Why not take one now, with your son," I suggested.

She nodded, clearly thinking the same thing. "Yes," she said excitedly. "If I could get away from work I'd be able to concentrate on him without all the other distractions. Maybe that would help us connect a little better. I don't really have a full vacation coming up, but I'll take one anyway. It's worth it!"

It was a small step, but an important one. If she could break the stranglehold of her competitive drive to take an impromptu vacation — placing her son's and her own needs above the demands of her career — she might eventually realize that her opinion of herself was more important than the image others perceived.

The proof that she had reached this point came not long after her vacation with her son. "You said I was using competition to escape competition," Brooke reminded me. "The more I thought about that, the crazier it seemed. I always assumed that you had to reach the top before you could relax and enjoy the people around you, before you could afford to be a nice guy. That's what my father always preached. But I can see now that I've never enjoyed being tough and abrasive, elbowing people aside so I could get ahead. What I really want is to be able to kick back and relax with the people around me, listen to their problems and ask their advice. So one day I decided to have all this out with my father, and I faced up to him for the first time in my life. I told him I am sick of trying to measure up to his scorecard, that I am finally going to cut loose and begin doing what I feel is right instead of what I think he would want. His reaction really threw me. He didn't know what I was talking about! He told me he has no scorecard, said he figured we could keep our own scores now that we're adults. He assumed I *was* doing what I wanted . . ." Brooke's voice faltered as she continued. "And he told me he loves me — whatever I do."

Breaking through the misperceptions that for so long had clouded her relationship with her father provided an enormous release for Brooke. In effect, it gave her the long-overdue permission she needed to accept and follow her own mature judgment. "At work people were pretty mistrustful when I began opening up," she reported. "After all, I've never been too forthcoming. But as I listened to the people around me, I heard this one fellow talking about what he wanted to do in his career. I realized that he was talking about just that — what he wanted to do, not what he wanted to be. He was a buyer, like me, but what he really enjoyed was marketing. He talked about the challenge, the creativity, the game of it, and I knew he honestly was attracted to the work and not just to what it might do for his career. The job that was being offered to me was in marketing, and the more I listened to him, the more I realized that I would never enjoy it as he could. I wasn't excited by it and I didn't want it. So I smoothed the way for him to take it instead. And you know what? I got more satisfaction out of that than just about anything I've ever done in my career. I felt relief and pride, and I also felt that for the first time I was doing something that felt right for me as well as my career."

"So where do you go from here?"

"For now, I'm still taking stock. On our vacation I allowed myself to hear another truth, which is that I can't just cut Jack out of my son's life. And I realized that the only reason I wanted to do that was because I needed to win. Now we're adjusting the custody arrangements so that Jack is back in the picture. At any rate, my son has priority for the moment. Meanwhile, I'm reassessing my career options too, trying to figure out what it is I truly like to do so that I can decide what I want to do next." She looked at me with a relaxed smile. "In a strange way, I consider my career even more important now. But it's not getting to the top that counts."

▼
WHAT'S YOUR
COMPETITION QUOTIENT?

What kind of a competitor are you? To find out, choose one response to complete each of the following statements:

1. When my friends begin to discuss politics
    a. I try to persuade the group to my point of view.
    b. I play devil's advocate to make the conversation more interesting.
    c. I don't really get worked up unless someone attacks my beliefs.
2. My friends tend to be people who
    a. have interests and lifestyles that are different from mine.
    b. are very similar to me.
    c. admire me.
3. In school I
    a. enjoyed learning about new ideas even when I didn't get good grades.
    b. only liked the classes in which I got A's.
    c. was able to enjoy a class as long as I didn't get less than a C.
4. If I got an A in school, I
    a. felt good about it only if it was a higher grade than anyone else received.
    b. felt good about it only if I'd worked hard to deserve it.
    c. always felt good about it.
5. My major career goal is to
    a. be widely respected in my field.
    b. keep learning and developing new skills.
    c. maintain a comfortable living and stay even with the competition.
6. I most enjoy being praised for
    a. doing consistently good work.
    b. doing a better job than others at my level.
    c. improving my performance.

7. I would like to
   a. equal my parents' standard of living.
   b. do what I love, even if it means having a lower standard of living than my parents.
   c. have a higher standard of living than my parents.

8. I would like my parents and siblings to
   a. be proud of me.
   b. be impressed by me.
   c. give me objective advice and criticism.

9. I am happiest when my partner
   a. challenges me to learn something new.
   b. takes up one of my interests.
   c. is content to let me be the expert.

10. My partner and I generally
    a. feel jealous of each other's advancement.
    b. try to help each other advance.
    c. don't care whose career does better as long as the bills get paid.

11. When I play a game, I
    a. quit if I start losing badly.
    b. put every ounce of energy into winning.
    c. like to have fun, whether I win or lose.

12. I prefer sports in which I
    a. play one on one.
    b. play on a team.
    c. am on my own.

13. I would like my children to
    a. be advanced enough to skip ahead in school.
    b. get good grades across the board but remain with their age group.
    c. excel in areas that interest them, even if it means doing less well in other subjects.

14. I feel it's most important for my children to
    a. see me as I am.
    b. respect me.
    c. model themselves after me.

15. When driving on a busy highway, I
    a. try never to get caught behind another vehicle.
    b. try to maintain a steady speed in the middle lane.
    c. pace myself against the other cars.

16. When there are long lines at the grocery store, I
    a. try to persuade the manager to open a new register.
    b. switch from line to line to find the fastest one.
    c. look at a magazine while waiting my turn.

17. When I see someone wearing beautiful clothes, I feel
    a. admiration.
    b. envy.
    c. resentment.

18. When I meet someone who is extremely fit, I
    a. want to challenge him or her to a contest or race.
    b. ask for suggestions on exercise and nutrition.
    c. try to make my regimen sound impressive.

19. My fashion sense is that of a
    a. trendsetter.
    b. eclectic.
    c. conservative.

20. My most important consideration when buying a new home is
    a. the socioeconomic level of the neighborhood.
    b. proximity to work, school, and friends.
    c. the look and comfort of the house itself.

▼

WHAT'S YOUR
COMPETITION QUOTIENT?

Evaluation

To find your competition quotient, locate your responses on the table below.

		COMPETITIVE TYPE (BY RESPONSE)		
Item	*Category*	*Type I*	*Type D*	*Type O*
1.	Friends	b	c	a
2.	Friends	a	b	c
3.	School	a	c	b
4.	School	b	c	a
5.	Career	b	c	a
6.	Career	c	a	b
7.	Family	b	a	c
8.	Family	c	a	b
9.	Relationship	a	b	c
10.	Relationship	b	c	a
11.	Sports	c	a	b
12.	Sports	b	c	a
13.	Children	c	b	a
14.	Children	a	b	c
15.	Behavior	c	b	a
16.	Behavior	a	c	b
17.	Appearance	a	b	c
18.	Appearance	b	c	a
19.	Possessions	b	c	a
20.	Possessions	c	b	a

If you are primarily Type O, you have a strong tendency toward offensive competition. If this runs through all areas of your life, or if it shows up mainly in your family and marital relationships and behavior, your competitive nature may be damaging your quality of life as well as your chances of personal happiness.

If you are primarily Type D, you are prone to defensive competition. Your cautious, conservative nature may help you advance in your career and maintain a stable home life, but it may also prevent you from taking the risks that contribute to personal growth. Your world may be secure, but you may not be giving yourself enough freedom to achieve internal success.

If you are primarily Type I, you are most responsive to incentive competition. You are receptive to new and different ideas and appreciate relationships that challenge you to grow. If *all* your responses came under this category, however, you may be cultivating idealism at the expense of pragmatism.

5

▼

THE PUSH
TO SPECIALIZE

*"If I don't start training for a profession in college, I won't
stand a chance of having a successful career."*

— Al, age 18, college freshman

TALK TO most college students today, and you will hear the
angst in their voices as they describe the future. "I need to start
specializing now," says a harried freshman, "so I can get a jump
on my major and graduate school. If I wait till I'm a sophomore
or junior to choose a field, it will be too late. I won't have the
edge I need to get ahead." Specialization, supposedly, is the
ticket to success, and no one believes this more than the young
people who flock to the doors of the nation's business, engineering, law, and medical schools each year. But the trend toward
specialization is not new, nor is it limited to recognizable professions. It is a cultural attitude that has been building for centuries.

Specialty is just another version of what used to be described
as a calling. Your calling may be parenthood, volunteer work,
executive management, painting, teaching, or repairing cars, but

106

in any case it is defined by one particular activity through which you earn recognition. If you consider your hobbies, sports, relationships, after-hours jobs, and personal passions to be peripheral — not determinants of success — then you specialize in work. In this respect, specialization is as much a function of priorities and values as of vocation.

The general concept of specialization dates back to the 1500s, when Protestant theologian John Calvin devised the notion of calling as an offshoot of his theory of predestination. Each of us, he maintained, is born with a certain assignment slated in our destiny, and by embracing this calling we contribute to the order of God's Universe. Wealth, he held, is one of the ultimate signs of rank in this Universe, the rich being among God's Elect. So not only should we limit the scope of our ambitions to a particular type of work, but we should direct those ambitions to earn maximum profit. Few of us today would justify our careers in terms of religious predestination, but many of the values that drive us are otherwise right out of Calvinist doctrine.

Since Calvin's time, the creation of ever narrower specialty fields has been propelled by industrialization, with its emphasis on assembly lines and bureaucracies, and by global competition. When the Soviets launched Sputnik in the 1950s, America responded with a push toward technological superiority that was felt from this country's classrooms to corporate boardrooms. Competition was the game, and specialization was to be our winning strategy. But on an individual and, arguably, a national basis, this approach has backfired. While we are encouraged to view work as a contest, we frequently focus on such narrow areas that we can easily lose sight of the larger whole. Our leaders hoped the further division of labor would produce proof of this country's global supremacy, but many Americans have become so mired in the minutiae and rivalry within their own specialty areas that the result is often more infighting than excellence.

The Western notion of specialization reflects a static view of the world and of human nature that may have seemed appropriate in Calvin's day but is glaringly out of sync with modern times. Specialization leaves individual needs unmet and obstructs personal change, largely ignoring changes in individual opportunity and market demand. If you accept the idea that you have but a single calling, you may end up feeling guilty and fearful should you find yourself longing to switch or branch out into other fields. You may be immobilized if your job becomes obsolete, despite the fact that many positions are doomed to obsolescence by changing technology or market demands. In these respects, specialization can be a straitjacket.

Nevertheless, we are told that Renaissance careers don't buy success in modern America but specialized careers do — and the narrower the focus, the greater the promised rewards. Doctors who treat a small area of the anatomy command far more prestige than general practitioners who treat the whole body. Lawyers who restrict themselves to a small area of the law are in greater demand than general counselors. Stock traders who handle only certain kinds of bonds, commodities, or mutual funds are more quotable than the brokers who buy and sell it all. The message is clear: if you want to get ahead, specialize.

Finding Your Track

The push to select a specialty and get on track begins even before college, particularly in upper socioeconomic classes. It dovetails with family desires for children to "do well," which often means aspiring to the parents' ambitions for them. Many youngsters are not simply encouraged to choose a general direction, they are assigned a career path and a future before they even realize that alternatives exist.

Of course, not all parents are pushy and not all youths malleable, but even if the job description remains open, the pressure to choose a specialty of some kind remains intense, particularly among the college educated. Despite the ostensible aim of the liberal arts education to provide a "rounded" foundation of learning, most students and their parents expect college to provide a practical foundation for earning. "What are you going to do with a degree in modern American literature?" a mother demands, glaring at her bemused daughter. "Why don't you study something *useful!*" Even if she balks at her mother's reprimand, when the daughter sees her friends scurrying off to their pre-med, pre-law, and pre-business classes, she may ask herself the same question.

Many of us chose our specialties less on the basis of genuine interest than fantasy, family pressure, opportunity, and above all, the promise of external success. Since one of the functions of a career is to enable us to pay the bills, it's sensible to select a profession for which there is an expanding market. The laws of supply and demand apply to jobs as well as to commodities. The more students allow the market to dictate their career choices, however, the more vicious the competition becomes. In recent years, for example, the nation's law schools have turned out so many young lawyers who are motivated primarily by money that there is less and less room for students who are primarily interested in the law. It's more difficult to get into law school and pass the bar, and there are fewer positions available to graduating lawyers. When the cycle completes itself, the passionate as well as the acquisitive pre-law student will feel compelled to choose another calling more in line with market demand.

Such pragmatic choices have a way of gaining momentum and ending up as unfulfilling career tracks. The boy who spent every spare moment tinkering with cars or inventing whimsical machines turns the corner into adulthood and never looks back as he leaves mechanics for the corporate climb that might one day net him a six-figure salary. The girl who dreamed of becoming a career diplomat accedes to her father's advice to major in economics, then emerges from college to accept a position at a brokerage house and exchanges her dreams for "reality." When you specialize for the sake of external success, it may be hard to keep your deeper passions alive. There is less time, less energy, and less encouragement to pursue interests outside your career track. Eventually you lose the necessary knowledge and skills, and the pursuits that you perhaps assumed you would resume after achieving career success gradually fade from view.

The great irony is that single-minded specialization rarely pays off in the long run, even in terms of external success. Corporate recruiters overwhelmingly specify leadership and interpersonal skills as the assets they seek in managerial candidates.[1] Increasingly, recruiters are finding these assets less prevalent among the specialty school graduates than among individuals with diverse backgrounds. The armed services and the Peace Corps, they say, are particularly fertile sources of tomorrow's business leaders. And while a narrow educational focus may buy a short-term salary advantage, liberal arts graduates tend to earn more over a period of years. They have more options in their careers and ultimately achieve higher positions, as well as greater job satisfaction. They are twice as likely as engineering graduates to end up in senior management within the corporate structure, and college graduates who majored in humanities or social sciences tend to progress throughout the business world in greater numbers than those with business degrees.[2] In tacit recognition of this fact, Harvard Business School's ultrasecret Century Club admits only students with a broad range of interests, including politics, religion, and the arts — students whose breadth of awareness qualifies them as future leaders.

Sociologists and economists now blame overspecialization for much of the bureaucratic waste, delay and, increasingly, inefficiency and high prices that confront our economy today. They forecast a mass trend toward what business consultant Paul

Hawken calls disintermediation, or elimination of middle-men — specialists — who typically operate between the consumer and the goods or services consumed. As early proof of this trend, Hawken points to the proliferation of versatile non-specialized professionals, such as midwives and paralegals, as well as the growth of consumer-direct organizations, such as home shopping services, self-help publications, generic products, and arbitration and mediation. If this trend does turn into a mass movement, many of the specialty degrees we routinely view as tickets to success may soon lose their market value.

Whatever the economic conditions, internal success requires a strong sense of direction, which is often confused with specialization. But while direction is open-ended and flexible, specialization tends to be rigid and confining. While direction requires a high degree of self-knowledge and confidence, specialization can create the illusion of assurance even if, deep down, you are not at all sure of yourself. It provides a clearly defined area of competence that can shield you from other risks and challenges while giving you a feeling of authority. The real allure of specialization, in some cases, may lie in its promises of security and identity. Unfortunately, such promises are not guarantees.

From Amateur to Professional

Recent graduates face pressure to establish professional status as soon as possible. Much of this pressure comes from the media's tendency to make national heroes out of wunderkinder who amass their first millions before the age of forty. Consider the hoopla that surrounded the elevation of Steve Jobs, Steven Spielberg, and Donald Trump to the ranks of the Rich and Famous during the early 1980s. Had they taken ten more years to build their careers, they would no longer have possessed that youthful mystique, and the media probably would have bowed respectfully and moved on. Instead, they drew maximum exposure, not because their achievements were necessarily worthier than those of other high-performing entrepreneurs or artists, but because they were young.

The pervasive attitude is that if you don't make it in your thirties, you'll never make it at all. By the time you're forty you'll be on your way out to pasture, and your shot at the big time will have passed you by. This desperate, rather pathetic vision of later life is a powerful inducement to postpone the peripherals, such as love, friendship, marriage, and interests outside your specialty, until after you make your fortune. Then, in theory, you can sit back, relax, and retrieve everything you've forsaken on the way to success.

Many popular "success" manuals echo this attitude in their recommended one-year, five-year, and ten-year plans aimed toward ascending levels of recognition. While goal setting and strategizing are essential to achievement of all kinds, term plans can become psychological traps. In embarking on a five-year plan you presume to know what you will want five years into the future — a chancy presumption at almost any time of life but especially during the early stages of your career. The more closely you adhere to your plan, the more you will resist opportunities that might lead in other, possibly more rewarding directions, and the less prepared you will be should unforeseen personal or economic forces interrupt your progress. Rigid career plans tend to encourage specialization while limiting direction.

The pressure to prove yourself while still young intensifies the levels of anxiety, depression, tension, and frustration you feel while working. It's as if time, as well as your human competition, is constantly looking over your shoulder. Each accomplishment is measured against the calendar, so that no matter how outstanding your performance, you're not satisfied unless you've beaten your deadline. If you fail to meet a deadline, the anger and humiliation can be crushing because so much of your ambition is riding on each round.

Even if you do score an executive position, make a fortune, or become a celebrity while still in your twenties or thirties, you may find it difficult to stay on top. It's impossible to sustain that initial momentum indefinitely, and the emotional letdown when it stops can be overwhelming. This is true at any age, but the younger you are when you "make it," the greater are your chances of falling, because you have less of a foundation to support you. Also, your buildup is likely to be exaggerated because of your youth. While you might receive less applause if you make your big splash at age forty or later, you may also have a stronger base, emotionally and professionally, to see you through the subsequent plateau.

If you take a longer view of your professional life, you may be less willing to make the personal sacrifices often associated with fast-track careers. Recognizing that you may not reach your peak earning power until you are forty or fifty, you may decide that you can't wait that long to get married or have a family or explore more personally satisfying sideline interests. The more time you give yourself, the more opportunities you are likely to seize, and the more fulfilling your life is likely to be. This is one way to protect yourself against the stagnation and insularity that can occur in a specialized profession.

It may also contribute to long-term career advancement. Sociologist Srully Blotnick, who monitored the professional and private lives of more than five thousand working men and women for over twenty-five years, concluded that the individuals who attained the greatest professional satisfaction *and* recognition in his sample were not those who had given their all to their careers but those who had satisfying personal lives, including marriages and families that mattered at least as much as and often considerably more than their careers.[3]

Strangely, the modern work world sets up a catch-22 situation that initially discourages and ultimately rewards versatility. Companies may hire workers to perform a single job but prohibit them from working or even investigating areas outside their immediate specialties. Like children instructed to color within the lines, they are pressured to conform unquestioningly to highly specific job descriptions. Yet those who thrive at the very top often have had a broad range of experience and positions, which enables them to communicate knowledgeably with members of their own organization at all levels as well as with leaders of other enterprises. Because they can maneuver comfortably in a variety of arenas, they feel less anxious about constantly proving themselves. This allows them to maintain an openness and innovativeness, a sense of wonder that traces all the way back to childhood and is often squelched by specialization.

Paul Hawken describes this little-recognized success tool in *The Next Economy.*

> When reading stories about many successful people in different fields — scientists, business persons, inventors — I have been struck by how many of them were essentially naive in many ways and, therefore, looked at problems with fresh, unprofessional eyes. When Buckminster Fuller was in the navy, he asked himself why the bubbles in the boat's wake were round. This might sound like a "dumb" question, but it led him to geodesic domes and hundreds of other discoveries.[4]

You Are What You Do

During group therapy sessions, I often conduct an exercise in which I ask each person to characterize himself or herself by finishing the sentence "I am ———." The vast majority respond by defining themselves by what they do for a living. Only rarely does someone say, "I am a human being," or "I am the father of three wonderful children," or "I am fascinated by astronomy." Instead I hear, "I am a lawyer," or a doctor, manager, housewife, or accountant.

A sense of personal limitation is inherent in such responses. In many cases, it can be traced back to childhood conditioning. The girl who is discouraged from learning any but domestic skills may feel incapable of pursuing challenges outside the home. The youngster who is routinely criticized and demeaned may either give up potentially rewarding pursuits or feel compelled to succeed very visibly to prove the parents wrong. The child who is groomed from an early age for a specific occupation may be so locked into that mold that no other pursuits are ever even considered. When these children grow up, they often embrace their professional labels as their identities because they feel that their entire worth is wrapped up in their work.

Our culture, too, encourages us to confuse personal identity with the professional or public roles we play. We routinely label one another by profession and use occupational achievement as a measure of status. We overemphasize the importance of job rank and position while disparaging the very parts of our lives that provide the most satisfaction. "I play the violin in my spare time," explains the man who began studying music at age six, "but I'm *really* a dentist." Such an apologetic view of your own life can produce a deep sense of emptiness and confusion. You would do better to ask yourself what you want to *do* with your life than what you want to be in life.

Todd was grappling with just such confusion when he entered therapy. At age thirty-eight, he was making upward of $70,000 a year and felt like a failure. The problem, in his mind, was his job as a sales rep, a position that he'd accepted right out of college and that had proven too lucrative to leave. He was good at selling and had such control of his territory that he had to work only three or four days a week, yet his job embarrassed him. A reluctant bachelor, Todd was shy and awkward around women because he didn't feel he had enough prestige to hold their interest. Still in close touch with most of his friends from college, he was painfully aware of how powerful and successful they had become. He was special enough to be their friend, he thought, yet he was still in a low-level job while they were busily taking over executive suites. The issue wasn't money but status. Todd felt stuck in the wrong specialty.

Todd's confusion could be traced in part to his middle-class upbringing. He remembered his father, a successful lawyer, saying, "You can make a lot of money as a plumber, but if you really want to *be* somebody, you've got to join the executives." Not long after imparting this wisdom, Todd's father died. Todd was just ten at the time, but he vowed some day to achieve the kind of success his father would have admired. His good intentions were complicated by his older brother's decision to follow in their dad's footsteps and go into law. Lacking the courage to compete in the same field, Todd felt he should find one of his own.

Although he was a mediocre student, Todd was a straight shooter and a good judge of character early on. He gravitated toward the guys in high school and college who showed the most promise and hoped their ambition would rub off on him. But while he developed enduring friendships with these future leaders, they could not give him the direction he needed. When he stumbled across the sales position posted in the college career placement office, he seized it as a temporary move, a way to pay the bills until he decided how to proceed with his career. Fifteen years later, he hadn't moved and his ego was in what felt like a terminal decline.

I asked Todd if anything outside work gave him a feeling of pride or satisfaction. Having heard him describe himself as an abject loser, I was surprised when he promptly answered this question with a nod and launched into a description of his house. It seemed that he had bought a ramshackle bungalow on a half acre of land for a bargain price several years earlier. The house was unlivable and the grounds had gone to seed, but that hadn't deterred Todd. Serving as his own carpenter and contractor, he remodeled the building and landscaped the garden. The results were stunning, and for the two years it took him to complete the project, Todd hadn't worried about his job description or even felt particularly envious of his high-powered friends.

"But now the house is finished," said Todd, sighing, "and I feel like a joke again."

"Can you tell me any other strengths you have?" I asked.

"Well, I'm a pretty good skier, I guess . . . but that doesn't count for anything."

"Why not?"

"It doesn't really have anything to do with who I am. I mean, for example, I can't very well go up to a woman and say, 'Hey, I'm a great skier, and what do you do?' That doesn't sound any better than saying I'm a salesman."

"So instead of talking about your work or your strong points, you say nothing?" I asked. Todd nodded glumly. "Can you explain why you feel so ashamed of your job?"

Todd considered a moment, then replied, "All my life, I feel as if I've disappointed people. When I was a kid I thought if I'd worked harder in school my father wouldn't have worried so much, and he might have survived. After he died I felt that I was disappointing my mother and brother because I just could never get my act together. I felt that I was disappointing my friends because I couldn't keep up with them as they zoomed up their corporate ladders."

"Have any of these people actually told you they were disappointed in you?"

"I guess not," he said thoughtfully. "They're all busy going in their own directions. I suppose if I were honest I'd have to say they probably don't care that much what I do. Not even my mother pressures me directly."

"Have you lost any of your friends because you didn't keep up, as you say?"

"No."

"And why do you feel your father would have been disappointed in you?"

"I guess because I'm not turning out like him. I'm just not the executive type."

"If you were — if you'd fought your way into a prestigious specialty just like your brother — would that make you happy? Would that make you feel that you'd earned your father's approval?"

As Todd pondered these questions a look of discovery spread across his face. "I always thought it would make me happy, but now that I think about my brother's life, I realize that's probably wrong. He chose Dad's profession, even the particular area of law that Dad specialized in. He graduated at the top of his class, got a position with a big-time firm. I've always thought of him as this huge success. But you know, he's not really happy. He's had two divorces. He's into cocaine. He always claims that's just the way it is on the fast track, but maybe there's more to it. Maybe it has something to do with the fact that he's done all this to prove himself to Dad — and there's no way of knowing if he has succeeded or not. Because Dad is dead."

I nodded. "I think you may be exactly right. Do you see yourself in this picture?"

Todd shrugged. "I guess I never really understood Dad's expectations well enough to follow in his footsteps. I heard him talk about title and prestige, so I've always accepted that those are important markers of success, but what do you *do* with success once you've got it? It makes you look good to everybody else, but I think maybe I've always been a little afraid I couldn't handle it internally. I never felt that I could compete with my father's success the way my brother has tried to do. Much as I envy them, I can't even compete with my friends."

"It sounds as though you've been much harder on yourself than your friends or family have been," I suggested. "Maybe it's time to erase those old tapes that keep telling you you've got to be something you're not."

Todd had taken the first crucial steps toward a personally meaningful definition of success. In the months that followed we took a closer look at the values he considered important, his general goals in life, his dissatisfaction with his work, and the various options available to him. Creating a sense of direction involved marrying Todd's personal strengths with an array of pursuits that would give him a sense of pride and pleasure. Professionally, he decided to go into real estate development, an occupation that would utilize both his salesmanship and his flair for selecting and revitalizing properties.

But Todd discovered that work was not his only source of worth. Being directed meant that he cared deeply about everything he did, including skiing, developing new relationships, and reading ancient history, a boyhood passion he'd rejected after his father died. Most important of all, Todd came to understand, he could stop trying to pigeonhole himself into the imaginary success mold that he'd constructed in his father's memory. He was finally free to achieve his own brand of success in all its diverse glory.

While many people derive great pleasure from their professional accomplishments, few can rely on work alone to provide complete fulfillment. By extension, this means that you may never be fully satisfied with your professional career if you've sacrificed everything else to support it. You need a certain amount of diversity to feel that you are a complete human being. You need to take as much pride and joy in your accomplishments at home and at play as you do in your job performance. You need to recognize that what you think, feel, and desire are as much a part of who you are as the title below your signature.

The Dangers of Specialization

Any misgivings about specializing early in life are usually swept aside by the argument that there will be plenty of time and opportunities for other interests later on and by the excitement of the quest. It is exciting to enter a specialized field. Just by qualifying, you feel that you have accomplished a great deal, that you are special. The fewer members there are in your specialty, the more special you feel, and the more eager you are to excel. But with increased zeal comes pressure. Because you know precisely whom you're competing against and what you have to do to get ahead, the heat of competition is far more intense than in a larger field in which your conduct is scrutinized less closely.

The competitiveness that pervades specialties has a particular edge because of the social infrastructure of these groups. In keeping with the notion that we are what we do, most specialties encompass not only jobs but personal friendships and hobbies. Entering a specialty can be a lifestyle choice that harks back to the cliques and clubs of school. That same aura of superiority and elitism permeates clusters of adult specialists. As Alvin Toffler wrote, describing the trend toward professionalization that began in the sixties, "Whenever the opportunity arose for some group of specialists to monopolize esoteric knowledge and keep newcomers out of their field, professions emerged."[5]

The more difficult it is to become accredited in a field, the more rarefied the lifestyle surrounding that specialty tends to become. People within a profession tend to think, speak, look, and act much alike, and the similarities increase within narrower subspecialties. Physicians say they can distinguish plastic surgeons from other doctors simply by personality type. Attorneys say they can separate trial lawyers from corporate lawyers just by looking at them. While it's true that you may possess such characteristics before you choose your profession, if you enter a specialty field you are bound to absorb many traits of your fellows and thereby come to resemble them even more.

Not only are you apt to share certain appearances with others in your field, you may also spend most of you time with your coprofessionals, even outside of work. Medical specialists, for example, may treat patients, but they frequently socialize only with other doctors or professionals in related fields. Show business personalities gravitate to other entertainers. Champion athletes hang out with other sports or media figures. Saying that common interests bond these groups overlooks the glaring fact of their exclusivity. The real bond is not professional interests so much as professional success; simply being an actor is not enough to gain access to a star's inner circle, but being another star might be. For many, the subliminal attraction of specialization is less the common ground within a group than it is the badge of superiority over other groups. We want to be recognized as special just as much in adulthood as in childhood, and if we're not sure we can gain this stature on our own, joining an elite group is still the next best thing.

The closed culture (language, rules, educational background) that evolves within most specialties reinforces their insularity. The greater your expertise, the less time and patience you have for people who cannot speak the language of your specialty or understand the idiosyncracies of your job. As you lose the habit of communicating with outsiders, you lose the inclination to try. This arrangement limits opportunities for relationships based simply on affection and trust. Indeed, it encourages relationships based not on trust but on direct competition within the field.

Underneath the superficial camaraderie of specialties there

lurks deep suspicion and hostility because you all have your eye on the same goals. This is not so obvious when you're starting out, but as you ascend the pyramid of power and the ranks begin to shrink, it's hard to avoid comparing notes on your colleagues' progress. There *is* a choice between cooperation and competition even at this stage of the game, but taking a cooperative approach may challenge the entire system of advancement within the field. Many professions routinely pit top performers against one another, forcing them to compete for high positions. Given this strange mix of insularity and competition, it is quite possible to be the most "successful" member of your specialty — and end up without a friend. If you don't reach the top, the competition and alienation of the climb may leave you feeling defeated and burnt out.

But the emotional risks of advancing within a specialty represent only one set of dangers. Others stem from the narrow, often rigid occupational focus that underlies specialization. In the current climate of corporate takeovers, factory layoffs, and economic volatility, such a restrictive focus can bring more risk than security.

Corporate shake-ups and economic uncertainty are undermining what organizational psychologists call the psychological contract between employee and employer. As recently as the seventies, loyalty, dedication, and concentration could buy job security and steady advancement. Management consultants affirmed that this tacit contract benefited the companies as well as the employees, and many firms extended themselves to maintain this policy. However, the business environment today is not so understanding. Global competition, technological change, government deregulation, and the constant threat of corporate raiders are forcing companies to reorganize and review priorities. Many firms streamline staffs and reduce overhead as part of an overall plan to deter takeover threats. When a takeover becomes effective, new owners who are more interested in short-term profits than running the business may sell off assets and fire staff without regard for employees' longevity, loyalty, or special skills. When firms merge, whole departments may become redundant, and again the result is layoffs. Managerial and professional ranks — specialists — can be hardest hit by corporate reshuffling. More than half a million such positions were eliminated in some three hundred of the country's largest companies between 1984 and 1988. Without fallback skills and interests, many specialists have nowhere to turn when their jobs are cut.[6]

If you have devoted your career to a single purpose for many years and are suddenly laid off, the psychological and emotional repercussions can be devastating. You may blame yourself. You may feel you have no control over your life. You may feel that everything you've done has been for naught. Most of all, you may wonder why on earth you never cultivated other options or developed more varied skills.

Finding a Place on the Specialization Spectrum

Even if our economic system were structured differently, few of us would have the energy or inclination to juggle multiple professions, but we all have the potential to be "Renaissance people." What's required is not genius or wealth but simply an open mind.

While some careers demand proficiency in a particular specialty field, few require complete submersion. You can avoid the dangers of specialization and still work within a narrow field if you simply keep yourself open to outside ideas, challenges, opportunities, and relationships. By the same token, the least restrictive job can turn into a specialty if you rely on work exclusively to supply friends, entertainment, stimulation, and gratification — to supply your identity.

As simplistic as this advice may sound, if you are used to viewing yourself as a specialist it is not so easy to branch out suddenly. The physician who always introduces himself as Dr. Jones may derive so much of his self-esteem from his title that he feels denigrated when people call him by his first name. Simply saying "I'm Jack Jones" may leave him feeling uncomfortably exposed, but his reaction indicates just how tightly his profession confines him.

It's not surprising that when your identity becomes so enmeshed with your specialty, breaking out can cause a backlash effect. The reaction may be to discard all rules. The dedicated husband and father who's spent twenty years designing optical lenses suddenly decides he can't stand his life, walks out on his wife, kids, and work, and enters a revolving door of short-lived jobs and affairs — all in the name of aimlessness that masquerades as freedom.

Another reaction is simply to trade specialties. The burned-out microbiologist decides that she'll feel more successful if she earns a big paycheck, so she trades her research career for one as an industrial consultant. After the initial thrill of motion involved in any career change, the same feelings of alienation and frustration set in. This pattern is all too common in a period when many of us look to sudden change as a solution to problems that require much more complicated and often less drastic measures. Srully Blotnick found that nearly 36 percent of the job changes that occurred within his sample over twenty-five years resulted in a pay decrease and lower job satisfaction.[7]

A third reaction is to attempt too much diversity too soon. The middle manager who chafes at the restrictions of his office and quits to start his own business may find himself with more than he can chew, yet struggle determinedly to wield total control over his new enterprise. In his haste to prove himself capable in all areas, he may end up an expert in none.

Versatility is valuable, but it has to be balanced by a strong sense of direction. One way to approach this balance is by creating a personal definition of success that places work in perspective. Most of us get a good deal of satisfaction and pride from our successes at work, whether it involves raising children, manufacturing cabinets, mediating labor disputes, or running a corporation. If succeeding at work becomes too important, however, the mounting fear of failure may make it impossible to accept risk or change, both of which are essential for growth — on the job and off.

It may be helpful to think of your life as a triangle, with your career, your family, and your personal needs as the three points.

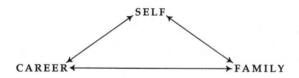

Each of these three parts of your life deserves equal attention and care. Unfortunately, the specialized culture within your firm or profession may overvalue work at the expense of family and self. Because all your colleagues show up at the office six days a week, you may feel obligated to do the same even though your work could be completed in five days. If you didn't, you fear, you might appear less ambitious or diligent than the others. Whether or not your fears are accurate, in trying to conform to such standards of conduct you may unwittingly cause the rest of your life to unravel, which in turn is likely to destroy your overall sense of direction.

If this is happening to you, you need to challenge the norms of your profession. Like Buckminster Fuller, give yourself permission to stop and examine the world around you without all the preconceptions and value judgments of your specialty. Consider what realistically will happen if you diverge from established patterns. Look for ways to achieve more balance within the system. Stop thinking in terms of what's expected of you and start reevaluating what you demand of yourself.

If your work environment is so rigid that there is no possibility of balance, you may need to review your personal goals and begin looking for alternative routes to achieve them. A job that forces you to submerge yourself in work leaves little room for fulfillment, but a job that allows you to enjoy both working and living allows you to be happy and productive.

DOES YOUR SPECIALTY
SUIT YOU?

It is difficult to feel happy and secure when your occupational identity is at odds with your personal identity. To determine how well you have integrated these two aspects of your life, complete the following steps. (This exercise may also be used to help you determine the suitability of a prospective job or profession.)

1. List the typical traits and characteristics of people in your occupation. Include the educational and personality standards, typical dress code, styles of behavior and appearance, and other general patterns you've observed among members of your field.
2. Review your list and identify the traits that you possessed when you first entered your profession.
3. Review your list and identify the traits that fit you now.
4. Consider the changes represented by these two inventories. Do you feel that the changes you've undergone since entering your field are compatible with your personal values and goals? Are you proud of these changes, or do you feel that you've compromised your true nature by conforming to the standards of your specialty?
5. If your responses indicate any of the following, you may need to reconsider your career choices.
   a. You possess few or none of the traits you've listed as typical of your profession.
   b. You feel that your occupation has caused you to change in undesirable ways.
   c. You feel that you were suited for your occupation when you entered the field, but either you or the field has changed so that you are no longer comfortable with your professional identity.

PART III

THE PRICE OF GLORY

SUCCESS AS A HABIT

"I can never really see myself as a success — no matter how much other people praise me. Every time I lose a case — even if I didn't stand a chance of winning — I feel it proves I'm a fraud."

— *Dana, age 31, lawyer*

WHEN YOU'RE BEGINNING your career, every pat on the back seems thrilling and every minor accomplishment points to your brilliant future. At first the occasional commendation gives you a genuine rush of satisfaction. The praise inflates your ego and boosts your self-esteem. It reassures you that you, too, are entitled to share in the American Dream. But soon you may begin to sense that simply earning a comfortable salary and receiving the odd acknowledgment is not good enough. To sustain a really satisfying high of attention and approval, you may feel compelled to prove yourself not just competent but superior.

It's as if you've qualified for the competition, but you still have to win round one, then two, then three, and on and on until you've reached the "top." Only then, it seems, will you finally believe that you are good enough. Only then will you feel free to direct your own destiny. Unfortunately, once you're hooked on external recognition, you may well never be free again. This kind of dependency can subtly distort your values and priorities, trapping you in a maze of illusions and blocking your way to deeper fulfillment.

Born to Succeed

Among the many success skills we possess from birth is a natural tendency to weed out challenges that are too easy or far too difficult and to embrace challenges that are barely within our grasp. Thus, we set ourselves up for accomplishment and learning by selecting tasks that force us to stretch without causing excessive frustration. The psychologist Nicholas Hobbs called this acceptable challenge zone the level of just manageable difficulty. A task that falls within this zone forces us to work at about 80 percent capacity to solve it. This is the optimal level of difficulty for steady progress. An occasional spurt of 90 percent capacity work may be exhilarating, and a brief descent to 60 percent can be relaxing, but pushing to work harder for an extended period can leave us feeling stressed and anxious, while a steady diet of easier tasks leaves us bored and restless.

This natural challenge gauge seems to be most accurate in early childhood. Place a two-year-old in a room filled with toys of varying difficulty and she will make a beeline for those which are just tough enough to challenge her. If a toy turns out to be too simple or too advanced, she will quickly discard it, but when she masters a particular toy, the achievement spurs her to aim just a little higher the next time around.

Regrettably, we don't always have the luxury of selecting our own tasks as we get older. School rarely offers choices of assignments. And while we do choose our professions, most jobs come with a mix of duties presenting varying degrees of challenge. Some teachers and bosses try to adjust their demands to individual skill and talent levels, thereby maximizing our chances for success, but few of us are allowed to make the steady, gradual progress that nature seems to have intended.

When we are repeatedly forced to take on challenges that we cannot master, our natural challenge gauge falters, and we start to view ourselves as losers. By as early as fourth grade, most children have labeled themselves, consciously or subconsciously, as successes or failures in particular school subjects. These labels may accurately reflect their past academic performance, but children who label themselves as failures do not accurately anticipate their future performance: they expect to fail in their problem subjects even when they are able to do well, so they continually lower their expectations — and reduce their options. Children who view themselves as successes in a subject, however, retain the ability to predict how well they will handle the next challenge: they expect to succeed most when they are in fact able to succeed, and so keep raising their aspirations in their "good" subjects.[1]

Fortunately, most of us find that we can excel in at least some aspects of our lives, and we tend to focus our ambitions on those areas. The more we continue to achieve, the more we discover that it genuinely feels good to master those just manageable challenges. But external success also brings recognition, approval, and money, which reinforce the desire to prove ourselves over and over. The exhilaration of winning adds competitive incentive to the habit. And the outside obligations that often accompany success — more expensive possessions, school tuitions, and a higher public profile — increase the external pressure to keep performing. With so many forces pushing us ever forward, it's easy to get rolling too fast.

Once we've acquired a reputation for success, we have to out-perform ourselves continually to keep upping the rewards and accolades. But as the stakes increase, the time frame shortens, and this further intensifies the pressure. Thus, after you've won that first promotion, your tendency is to target a position much farther up the ladder while setting a shorter deadline within which to reach it. If you "reward" yourself for your promotion by pur-chasing a new car or home (with hefty mortgage payments), having a child, planning an expensive vacation, or otherwise raising your expenses, financial obligation will underscore that deadline. Simultaneously, you may begin to demand more of yourself in your private as well as professional life. Having won one at work, you may feel compelled to prove yourself a winner in other areas, too, and so become a competitive athlete, dieter, parent, or socialite.

This frenzy of competitive pressure leads to a predictable breaking point, however, when the pace of achievement out-strips capacity: the level of challenge moves beyond 80 percent capacity, up to the 90 or 100 percent range. Not only does this make life increasingly stressful, but it increases the likelihood of failure. The logical conclusion of this process, of course, is the familiar Peter Principle: that each person tends to rise to the level of his or her incompetence.

Despite the tendency to keep raising the stakes, we benefit from our accomplishments most when they build slowly on each other. The person who resists the temptation to play beat the clock and manages to stay within the 80 percent challenge zone may be able to attain great prominence without ever succumb-ing to the Peter Principle. The rewards are most satisfying when success is an ongoing process that is accented but not domi-nated by individual triumphs. Problems typically occur when one singular achievement suddenly preempts all the rest.

The Big Win raises the stakes too abruptly, setting unrealistic new standards and making it nearly impossible to build from this milestone as we have from previous ones. It is the reason many authors experience severe writer's block after one of their books becomes a best seller. Such authors tend to be more sensitive to poor reviews of subsequent books than they were to criticism of their earlier work. Even lottery winners who become overnight millionaires often lose their motivation to work or set goals for themselves, and they find less real satisfaction in their new luxury than in their former lives.

When you experience a big win that lifts you to the top of the external success ladder, your anxiety over failure tends to increase for two reasons. First, the more you achieve, the more you have to lose — and the more people will notice when you do. And second, the big win may feel so unreal to you that you cannot believe you deserved it. Naturally, then, you assume that your next effort will be far less impressive — and look like a failure by comparison. At the same time, though, you may feel such emotional and social pressure to duplicate your accomplishment that the heightened risk of failure can be truly agonizing.

At the root of this anxiety is a misunderstanding of success as the absence of failure. Whether the compulsion to achieve stems from early childhood conditioning or later societal pressures, the net result is that failure is equated with disgrace. In fact, though, failure is a vital component of progress. Discovery is born from experimentation, which in turn is born from the willingness to risk failure. Scientists understand the value of failed experiments as a source of information and perspective. It is not a matter of rationalizing mistakes but of utilizing them. All too few of us have the courage or confidence to apply this same attitude to mistakes we make in our personal and professional lives. Instead, we try to disavow our errors and put them behind us as quickly as possible. Rather than viewing them as opportunities, we treat them as obstacles. The next time around, we may run from risk altogether or blindly stumble into the same mistakes all over again.

We commonly reward ourselves with a "well-earned rest" after major accomplishments, and penalize ourselves by working even more frantically when we've fumbled. This arrangement is counterproductive. Typically, right after a grand success, our motivation, self-confidence, and momentum are at a high point, making us eager to take on the next challenge. With the exception of overachievers who are already operating at 90-plus percent capacity, most of us do not need to break the momentum at this point. Even after a big win, it's usually best to maintain a normal routine until the emotional sizzle subsides. The specter of failure looms largest, after all, when we feel like moving forward but instead stand still. The time to take stock comes later, when the win can be viewed in context.

When we do need to step back and reflect is after major setbacks. Failure depletes our self-confidence and strength and stops our momentum cold. We may feel compelled to redeem ourselves as quickly as possible, but trying to press ahead after a major upset is like attempting a marathon with a sprained ankle. The more we push ourselves, the more likely we are to fail again, perpetuating the downward cycle of performance and frustration. By stopping to analyze our failures, we prevent the downtrend and give ourselves the chance to regain perspective and confidence. Instead of reacting automatically, then, we can reassess our direction and strategy, taking into account the mistakes of the past. This revitalization process increases the likelihood of success on the next round and diminishes the damage done by each individual loss.

The Promotion Trap

Even when the success habit does not lead to incompetence, it can lead to disillusionment and dissatisfaction. Because external recognition and approval feel so good, and because we are conditioned to believe we must keep improving our image to reap those rewards, we can easily get caught in a progression that raises our status while diminishing our intrinsic satisfaction.

Cheryl found herself in just this sort of bind after being awarded the job of executive director of a national consumer organization. She'd been with the organization for fifteen years, starting as a researcher and moving into lobbying and outreach as she rose through the ranks. Cheryl knew the issues, strategies, and leaders inside out, and at thirty-seven she seemed well qualified to head the organization. The problem was that each advancement up the ladder seemed to be taking her farther and farther from the work she really loved: exploring problems and developing solutions. She excelled at everything she did, so it had been taken for granted that she would rise to the top. But having allowed herself to get swept up in the standard progression of promotions, she had not given adequate thought to her personal values, ideals, and interests.

When she began her career in the early seventies, Cheryl was a committed political activist, and the organization had provided her with hands-on training in everything from occupational and environmental safety to governmental reform. On the research staff, she had worked on projects with scientists, politicians, and students. She had never yearned for a big paycheck or prestige; it was exciting enough to help guide a movement that she felt was vital to the nation's future.

Cheryl felt the movement was as vital as ever, and she appreciated the recognition that had landed her in a position of leadership. What dismayed her were the tasks at hand: fund-raising, public speaking, smoothing the ruffled feathers of board members and volunteers. Theoretically, she was the guiding force behind the organization, but in reality her administrative and fund-raising tasks left her little time to focus on the key issues, much less the policies for dealing with them.

When Cheryl came to me with her dilemma, she was convinced that there was something wrong with her.

"This is a great job!" she insisted after describing the position. "If I can just stick with it, I'll have the credentials and reputation to move in any direction I please. Why am I so miserable?"

"From what you've told me," I replied, "it's not the job but the title that impresses you. Anyone who works in a hierarchical organization can make the same mistake. You were led to believe that this position is the best because it's located at the top of the pyramid and because it commands the highest salary and the most respect and power. You might have spared yourself this confusion if you'd been allowed a trial run in the director's seat fifteen years ago, but that's not the way hierarchies work. They tend to glamorize positions of authority so that the most qualified individuals will want to rise to the top. Unfortunately, as you've discovered, the most qualified candidates do not always make the best authority figures — not if their *personal* goals point in a different direction."

Cheryl looked thoughtful. "I'm not sure my personal goals conflict with my having authority. They do conflict with the job description."

"If that is the case, you might consider using your authority to adjust your job description."

Cheryl's face lit up. She had been wrestling with two alternatives — plodding on in the job as it was or quitting and going back into research — neither of which appealed to her. At the suggestion of a third possibility, her creative wheels began to turn.

"I could split my job in half, effectively creating a new position for myself," she said, planning out loud. "If I offered to halve my salary too, the board would approve it. We could hire someone with experience in administration and fund-raising to be the director, and that would leave me free to concentrate on policy issues and networking with government agencies and corporations."

Cheryl had mistakenly assumed that her unhappiness stemmed from a problem within herself. She had never questioned the standards of a bureaucracy that ranks success according to position, salary, visibility, and contribution to the bottom line. Once she realized that there was another way to formulate success, according to her personal skills and priorities, she felt she'd regained control of her career. She would have to make some sacrifices, but they were no more severe than the ones she'd made throughout her professional life. The real difference was that these sacrifices would allow her to realize her own concept of success *now* instead of perpetuating the system's distant illusion of fulfillment. Having granted herself permission to manage her career creatively according to her personal values, she was much freer to set a pace and challenge level that would enhance both her external performance and her internal satisfaction.

Beating the System

To fully understand how Cheryl could be hoodwinked by her organization's hierarchy, you may find it helpful to consider how your own views of success have been influenced by the "system." Your first taste of the system was school. You were part of that system, along with your classmates, teachers, school administrators, grades, assignments, and rules. How well you handled — or manipulated — all those other elements determined whether you succeeded.

The view of success as a system-dependent product rather than a personal process not only undermines intrinsic motivation but encourages many students to try to beat the system — to advance by manipulation instead of scoring on the merits. Those who manage to do to this in school often try the same tactics in the workplace. The result may be unethical and sometimes criminal conduct. Having conned his teachers to get a good grade, the brash young manager tries to con his boss into giving him a promotion. Having been conditioned to fight for grades, the junior systems analyst refuses to share credit or even to recognize other people's contributions to group projects at work. Having impressed her youthful friends by circumventing rules in school, the novice salesclerk tries to win over her coworkers by outwitting her supervisors, lying about her experience, and stealing time off. Having used his family's connections to secure his acceptance into the finest boarding schools and college, the ambitious young politician uses the same pull to secure his election to the state senate. The fact that such maneuvers may initially be overlooked or even rewarded supports the notion that it pays to beat the system.

In his long-range study of working men and women, Srully Blotnick concluded that those most likely to use shortcuts and rely on personal image rather than diligence are in their twenties, a period normally filled with experimentation and role playing anyway.[2] Because our culture places such an emphasis on "making it" young, recent graduates sometimes feel compelled to use shortcuts. These inexperienced youthful offenders rarely understand that cutting corners produces only short-term illusions of competence — and few of us can manufacture long-term satisfaction out of illusion. They genuinely believe that cheating is expected behavior. When they eventually are found out, they may lack the skills and principles to redeem themselves.

Later in life, unethical conduct is used less often as a shortcut to success than as a desperate attempt to stave off failure and save face. Put another way, it is not a ploy to beat the system but a last-ditch effort to survive within the system. The healthiest reaction to failure is to scale down and choose a more attainable goal, which is precisely what we did as children when faced with too difficult a task. It is what our internal challenge gauge tells us to do. Yet this healthy impulse is often overridden by the stigma attached to failure. After all, many of us are conditioned from early childhood to believe that the world belongs to winners, that losing is a sign of weakness, and that failure brings disgrace. In school we learned to be ashamed of mistakes and, by extension, to hide them, but rarely to value and learn from them. This in turn encouraged the use of manipulation and even dishonesty as a tool of advancement.

So instead of scaling down our goals to a more manageable level, we may struggle to avoid failure by any available means — even cheating, theft, bribery, or violence — if the price of failure is high enough. Much of white-collar crime follows this pattern: a law-abiding businessman works hard to build an impressive career but finds himself with a crisis he can't handle and, rather than admit weakness or accept bankruptcy, breaks the law. In this respect, the habit of success can be as hazardous as the drug habit that forces an addict to kill and steal.

Inevitably, the success habit and the attitudes and conduct that support it spill into social and family relationships. If you cut corners and misrepresent yourself at work, you may find yourself lying and shortchanging your responsibilities at home as well.

Robert had slipped into just such a downward spiral years before I began seeing him. At age thirty-two, he had a ten-year record of outward success, but his family was disintegrating, he was plagued by migraines, and his business was in trouble. As in many such cases, Robert's problems could be traced back to his mother, a local politician, and his father, a corporate president. Robert, who was raised in the prep school and country club circuit, never questioned his duty to live up to the family's reputation. Misreading the deep disturbances that ultimately ruptured his parents' marriage, Robert assumed the family was healthy and normal and that his parents' professional achievements were a unifying force. He was proud of his parents and believed that they were proud of each other. He wanted them to be proud of him. The trouble was, though they claimed they wanted to be proud of him and his sister, Robert never felt that he really had his parents' approval. And the more they withheld it from him, the harder he strived to satisfy them in the only way he knew, by rivaling their professional accomplishments.

By the time Robert was twenty-two, his determination was paying off. He was the whiz kid of the bond market, earning sky-high commissions and putting in sixteen-hour days as a broker. He worked off tips from old schoolmates, operating throughout the business community. He called it networking. His parents encouraged him. His sister, an unpublished writer, envied him. His boss promoted him. Robert figured that he was born to succeed.

In short order, Robert married his high school sweetheart, another prep school veteran with the proper social cachet, and they produced a baby. It was time, Robert decided, to take the next step toward becoming a captain of industry. With his father's help, he bought his own company, a small shoe factory.

Having established his reputation for success, Robert was under tremendous pressure to perform as a tough, smart entrepreneur, but he had neither the qualifications nor the talents he needed to excel at his new venture. So he lied, telling his family everything was going well. He tried to con his customers and his creditors into trusting him. He toyed with the balance sheets until they looked impressive. And he cut corners on expenses by downgrading the quality of materials, thus cheapening his product. At the same time, he insisted he was upgrading quality and raised his prices. Robert was so determined to beat the system that he failed to notice that he had become the system he was beating! He was now the authority figure, and all these attempts to circumvent responsibility were destined to sink him.

But Robert's business problems weren't what brought him to my office. It was Mary, his wife, who'd insisted he start therapy, because after nine years their marriage was in trouble.

"Mary's in a rage because I don't spend enough time at home," Robert asserted. "But what I am supposed to do? Everything will be fine when I get the business running smoothly."

"It doesn't sound as though that's going to happen in the near future," I pointed out. "In fact, it may never run as smoothly as you'd like. I think you're avoiding the real issue here."

"Oh?" he said warily. "What is the real issue?"

"Your priorities," I replied. "Your business seems to be more important to you than your marriage, and your wife seems to know it."

Robert responded to that remark like a caged animal. He looked around the room, avoiding my eyes. He tapped his foot nervously. When he finally replied, the words burst forth in an explosion of defiance.

"What the hell does she want! I'm working my ass off to keep up with the credit card bills she racks up every month. She practically lives at the club, anyway. Hell, she's got the life she bargained for. I'm the one who's getting torn apart here."

"It sounds as if you're overwhelmed," I said. "Have you considered finding a partner or associate to help take some of the load off you?"

Again, that caged look. "I couldn't trust anyone else enough to share the control," he said. "I took on this challenge, and I'm going to make it work. I'm going to make it work big. I was brought up to be a winner, and I'm going to make my company a winner."

"Nothing's going to get in your way," I added, and he nodded vigorously. "Not even if it means sacrificing your family?"

"Listen," he said, his voice dropping to a beleaguered plea. "I'm doing everything I can to keep the ship afloat. There are only so many corners I can cut."

That comment revealed a great deal about Robert's underlying problems, both at work and at home. Instead of selecting personally meaningful goals and pursuing them straightforwardly, he had shouldered what for him was an unbearable load and assumed roles to impress everyone but himself. Overwhelmed by the constant grind of minor crises, he was oblivious to the long-term consequences of his conduct. And sustaining his heroic facade was so important to him that he refused even to entertain the thought of lowering his sights or allowing someone to share the burden. Instead, Robert cut corners, cheating his company of the strong leadership it required, cheating his wife of the intimacy and companionship she needed — he eventually confessed that he was having an affair — and cheating his child of the support and guidance she deserved. All this to preserve the captain-of-industry image that he hoped would prove once and for all that he measured up.

For Robert, recovery would require an unprecedented degree of honesty. After years of adjusting the facts of his life to fit his fantasies, he had to admit that his perceptions, his parents, and to a large extent his values were wrong. He needed to reevaluate his goals, assume responsibility for his actions, and make a commitment to his internal success and integrity for the first time in his life.

For anyone with Robert's background and conditioning, the changes required for recovery can provoke great anxiety. For Robert, the terror was so enormous that he backed out of therapy before he could even begin the process. Rather than admit that he probably could never win his parents' approval or that he had been largely living a lie, he arranged for therapy to become part of the system he was trying to beat. At first he simply failed to show up, but he paid the bills and told his wife he was continuing. Then, when his business crumbled around him and his wife began pressing for divorce, he disappeared. Ultimately it was easier for Robert to drop out altogether, to start living an entirely new lie, than to face his own reality.

Most people want a reputation for honesty, fairness, kindness, and generosity, but the pressures of competition tend to subvert honor. The most well-intentioned among us can get sucked into the belief that the ends justify the means, especially when the ends include the promise of personal validation. When more attention is paid to results than to the methods used to achieve them, questionable and even illegal tactics can seem irresistibly attractive. In time these tactics can become as habitual as the quest for external success itself.

The Marilyn Monroe Syndrome

External success can undermine your sense of worth and security if you adopt it as a personal identity. By definition, to get to the top you have to move above and apart from other people, which necessarily involves a certain degree of emotional isolation. Yet at the same time you may feel stripped of your individuality, because in struggling to satisfy external merit or status requirements you can sacrifice much of what matters most to you personally. On your own, then, you may find it difficult to relax and enjoy yourself, and the slightest setback may threaten your sense of self. Caught between your doubts and the exalted image others see, you can end up feeling like a fraud even if you rightly deserve every award or promotion you've ever received. I call this the Marilyn Monroe syndrome because, like the actress's tragic career, the lives of many powerful and prestigious celebrities are dominated by anxiety, depression, frustration, and under it all, the sense of being a fake.

Psychologists who have researched this phenomenon say that while men and women are equally prone to view themselves as success impostors, introverted people are most vulnerable.[3] The source of the problem can be traced to conflicts about success in childhood. If your teachers routinely praised your schoolwork while your parents insisted you were not working up to your potential, you may have been prevented from developing an accurate sense of your own accomplishment. On the other hand, if your natural talents and interests helped you to achieve excellence in a field that your family didn't condone or understand — if you were expected to become a scientist like your parents but instead soared in drama — you may have gotten caught between your own achievements and the family's aspirations for you. Both types of conflict can cause a rift between your perceived self-image (how you actually see yourself) and your externalized image (how you think others see you). The greater this rift, the more likely you are to view yourself as a fake. The more important your externalized image is to you, the harder you will try to live up to it — and the more anxious you will feel about being yourself.

A handful of people can sustain a diet of constant victory without sacrificing fulfillment. Usually part of the secret lies in not caring so much about winning but concentrating instead on the intrinsic rewards of work. The more you enjoy a task, the better able you are to concentrate and perform. Once external success becomes a central part of your identity, however, you have to care more about winning; if you don't win, your very being is threatened. Your passion for the work itself inevitably wanes under this pressure, but so does the thrill of winning, because each triumph only sets up another contest; if you bow out of the competition, you lose your identity.

Once caught in this syndrome, you may demand perfection of yourself even when no one else does. One of my patients, a thirty-one-year-old lawyer who earns more than $100,000 a year, was dismayed by her embarrassed and awkward performance at her first court trial. Before it was over she was saying that she should get out of law because she was a "failure." She was so dependent on success that she crumbled at the first glimmer of weakness in herself. To her, it proved what she had always suspected: that she was a fake. Had she been less obsessed with her reputation as a winner and more confident of her substantial abilities, she might have viewed the trial for what it was — a new opportunity for growth and self-discovery. Instead, she saw it as a pass-fail test.

If you are driven to win, you may devalue your past accomplishments and sometimes forget them entirely in a subconscious attempt to keep the pressure on future gains. As realistic as you may be in other areas, you may have a blind spot about yourself. In fact, the further you advance in the world, the less willing you may be to view yourself as a success, for fear complacency will set in. This subconscious standoff between what you do and how you see yourself has the effect of canceling the past so that you are forever starting over and looking ahead. It's a neat trick for maintaining momentum, but it produces a world without milestones or tangible results — and a life without satisfaction. No matter how much wealth or recognition you may receive, it's never enough because, in effect, you're afraid that success will be the end of you.

Aside from the tragic sacrifice of self-esteem and fulfillment, this arrangement leaves you dangerously exposed in the event of a serious personal or professional setback. Most of us comfort ourselves by looking backward, reviewing and savoring past moments of triumph, passion, joy, and pride. If you routinely wipe the slate clean after each of these moments, you deny yourself these memories. The loss of a job, your health, or a family member, then, may leave you devastated. Mid-life, which is normally a time of reflection and reassessment, may bring a profound sense of emptiness as you realize that you've thrown your life away for the sake of achievements you can't enjoy.

Another way your subconscious may work against you is by throwing the credit away. Instead of acknowledging to yourself that you deserve the praise you receive, you may unwittingly deflect it. If you're a workaholic, you may attribute your progress to your diligence rather than your competence. "I've gotten

147

to this point because I'm willing to put everything into it," you may tell yourself smugly. But what you may really be saying is that you're so sure you would otherwise fail that you overcompensate. If you don't feel that you've worked very hard, you may give the credit to luck, good looks, or charm — anything but the talent, skill, and intelligence that would make you a bona fide success in your own eyes.

The Marilyn Monroe syndrome sets up a no-win contest between achieving and failing. If your career falters or dives, it only validates your view of yourself as a fraud. If you progress, you may live in constant fear that your luck, looks, or energy will dwindle and that you will be found out. If your career soars, catapulting you into the company of superstars, you may feel guilty as well as anxious. If the levels of celebrity and guilt are high enough, you may unwittingly try to undermine your achievements by acting out. Richard Dreyfuss described the beginning of his personal decline, which occurred after he had starred in a series of blockbuster movies that culminated in an Academy Award for *The Goodbye Girl* when he was thirty: "I had enormous guilt feelings about how easily things had come to me and I started to resist the position I was in by drinking a lot, doing drugs, eating too much, being childish, denigrating my talent, and generally doing a lot of things that were getting in my way."[4] Sometimes it seems easier to self-destruct than to live as a pretender to greatness.

The Human Shell

Although we all are conditioned to think we want prominence, prestige, and wealth, many of us subconsciously view external success as a price we must pay for something far more fundamental, like love, respect, self-esteem, or autonomy. When the pursuit of material success becomes habitual, it's often because we are missing these vital sources of fulfillment. The illusion is that achievement will open them up to us.

The absence or weakness of these core resources can be traced to conflicts during childhood. Youngsters who do not receive the necessary foundation of unconditional love, respect, and discipline generally blame themselves for not "earning" their parents' support or for losing that support by acting out childishly. The misguided guilt and despair that arise out of such assumptions may be channeled into a passion for achievement. Material success, then, becomes a penalty for the real and imaginary crimes of youth, such as failing in school or otherwise defying family expectations. If I become wealthy or prominent enough, the adult child believes, it will make up for whatever I did that turned my father (or mother) against me, and I will be loved and feel good about myself again. In such a case, professional ambition is actually a form of self-castigation.

The struggle to gain parental acceptance is not always conscious or direct. Lingering family conflicts tend to infiltrate relationships later in life, and they may persist even after the parents have died. If you harbor this kind of unresolved conflict, you may transfer the parental role to your spouse or superior at work. You then work to gain your parents' approval by striving to please your replacement parents. In this scheme of things, whenever a task is not actively rewarded with praise, money, or a promotion, you perceive it as worthless — a failure. Yet the approbation you do receive never really satisfies you or sets you free because it does not resolve the underlying conflict.

Betsy had been jousting with "success demons" for more than twenty years before she realized how desperately unhappy her life had become. On the surface, she had it all. At work she'd been promoted to a senior-level executive position following the successful launch of a new product line under her direction. Her husband, Steve, was an accountant with his own firm. They had been married for eighteen years and had three children, ranging in age from eighteen to four, who were supervised by a live-in nanny. The family lived in a large Victorian estate in a wealthy suburban community where most of their neighbors were corporate executives. No one, not even her husband or her parents or children, could fathom why Betsy suddenly fell into a severe depression in the winter of her thirty-eighth year.

In fact, Betsy had been experiencing overt symptoms of distress and dissatisfaction for more than a decade. While she appeared to be gregarious and competent before her various audiences at work and at home, she spent much of her time hiding from those audiences. She relished the anonymity of her hour-long commute to and from the office. She immersed herself in the newspaper and business publications and spent hours each day planning her investment strategies. When she couldn't justify hiding behind a periodical or her desk, she turned on the television — anything to avoid facing her gnawing discomfort.

Nevertheless, Betsy could not trace the sources of her despair or specifically pinpoint anything wrong. It was more of an amorphous, creeping sensation, as if she were slowly being smothered. She felt increasingly detached from her children, cold toward her husband, and mistrustful of her coworkers. Having played the strong, bright model of efficiency ever since she dropped out of college to have her first child, Betsy no longer could remember what she was striving for. Perhaps more significant, she could no longer pretend that her achievements made her happy.

Betsy first appeared in my office at Christmastime. She was carrying a large bag filled with wrapped presents she'd just bought for her children, but her face lacked any trace of Yuletide joy. A tall, slightly heavy woman, she slumped in her chair and responded in an empty monotone when I observed that she'd been shopping.

"I used to get very excited about Christmas," she mused. "I spent a fortune on toys for the kids. On Christmas Eve I'd stay up practically all night building dolls' houses and making reindeer noises." She smiled vaguely. "This year I feel that I'm just going through the motions."

"It sounds as if you'd like to revive that feeling of excitement," I responded. "Tell me what aspects of Christmas you enjoyed most."

"It seems so stupid now, but I had a great time just playing. Once a year I felt as if I were one of the children, instead of the parent."

"What was Christmas like when you were growing up?"

Betsy thought for a minute. "It was definitely the best time of the year. I was the oldest of four girls. My parents ordinarily were pretty absorbed in their own lives. My father was away at work most of the time, and my mother started her own business when I was eight, but at Christmastime everyone was home and did things together. There were parties and we made cookies. Everyone helped trim the tree. School was out, so nobody worried about grades at Christmas. It was the one time when we could sleep late and do what we wanted."

I detected a note of longing in her voice. "Your parents demanded a lot of you?" I asked.

"They didn't demand, exactly, but they expected more than I was ever able to produce. I was kind of a problem student, and my father especially couldn't believe that any daughter of *his* could do as badly as I did in school. Naturally I always felt it was the teachers' fault. My mother sided with me and got me into a private school where it was harder to slip through the cracks. I still had trouble, but by high school I didn't care as much because I was able to work. I tried all sorts of different jobs and made quite a bit of money. My dad was proud of me for that. I figured it wouldn't matter if I never went to college, but was I wrong! Both my parents were determined for me to go. We must have applied to twenty, and one finally accepted me — a little college in the Midwest that no one ever heard of."

"Did you want to go?"

"I guess so. I mean, I wanted to get away from my parents, and it was a nice school with a pretty campus, but I felt very lonely when I got there. I missed Steve a lot . . ."

"The same Steve who is now your husband?" I asked.

"Mm." She nodded, knitting her brow. "Maybe if I had pushed myself to get more involved at college, he wouldn't be." She looked up. "It was a shotgun wedding, the summer after my freshman year."

"Tell me about it," I urged, suspecting that Betsy's problems could be traced, at least in part, to her marriage.

"There's not much to tell. I got pregnant. Our parents were mortified. I didn't think I could handle an abortion, and I didn't really want to go back to college either, so Steve and I got married. We always said we would have gotten married anyway, but I just don't know . . ." Her voice trailed off.

"You sound as though you now regret your decision."

"Eighteen years," Betsy said vaguely. "Time has just kept plowing on. Seems that if we've made it this far, there must be something holding us together."

"But you're not sure what that is?" I said, completing her thought. She shook her head. "What attracted you to Steve in the beginning?"

"He was clearly going to be somebody. He's very bright and has tons of drive. He seemed to know what he wanted, and he seemed to want me to be part of it."

"What was it that he wanted?"

She looked surprised. "Why, exactly what we have. A big house, expensive cars, pretty children, a successful wife."

"He wanted you to be a success?"

"Sure. He insisted I go to work soon after our first child was born, to support us while he finished school. After he graduated, he saw that I was moving up the ladder and insisted I keep on working. The fact that I was making good money impressed him."

"Just as it impressed your father," I observed. She raised an eyebrow at the suggestion, but nodded. "What did you want?"

"I'm not sure. I felt that I'd failed and disappointed a lot of people by then. I could never look my parents in the eye if I'd forced Steve to give up school too, and since I'd grown up with two working parents I knew my daughter would survive. At least if I earned a decent income I'd have a chance of making them proud of me."

"Like when your father praised you for earning your own money in high school," I suggested. Betsy nodded. "Did you *enjoy* working, though?"

She seemed perplexed by that question, as if she'd never considered it. "It didn't make any difference whether I did or not. I had to work at least until Steve got established as an accountant, and by then I had a shot at an executive position with my company. I knew I'd never have another opportunity like that." I thought I detected a note of shame in her voice as she added, "Not without a college diploma."

She shook her head and let out a deep breath. "Maybe I wasn't ready for school when I went. I certainly don't regret having any of my children. But I don't think I ever really had a chance to find my *own* source of inspiration. If only I'd finished college, I'd at least know what options exist for me!"

"And yet you have an executive position," I pointed out. "Doesn't that give you some sense of accomplishment?"

"My parents are thrilled. Steve says he's very proud. My kids boast about their successful mother."

"Yes, but how do *you* feel?"

She lowered her face and mumbled, "Empty."

"Are you saying you don't value your achievements?" I asked, trying to get Betsy to clarify her feelings.

"I'm not really sure what I value," Betsy sighed.

Before she could become whole, she would have to recognize how deeply those early parental accusations of failure and inadequacy had scarred her and how, by striving to fulfill her parents' and husband's expectations, she had actually been punishing herself. She then had to give herself permission to stop living according to their definition of success and start developing a personally meaningful definition of success. This would entail a careful examination of her own strengths and dreams and an honest appraisal of the parts of her life that gave her genuine pleasure as well as those that stirred her resentment and regret. Finally, she would have to confront her husband, children, parents, and coworkers and break the habit of success that had ruled her life for more than twenty years.

This is not an easy or quick process. It took nearly two years for Betsy to fully realize how few of her life decisions had truly been her own, and then to begin exploring what she had to change to recover a sense of meaning and importance. But the most difficult hurdle came at the end of this period, when she revealed her discoveries to her family. Mustering her courage, Betsy announced that she was going to leave her job and her handsome salary so she could go back to school for her bachelor's degree and spend more time with the children. Her parents informed her that she was too old to start over. Her husband groused about the loss of income and warned her that her decision might cost them their house. Only the children seemed pleased that she was no longer depressed and that they would see more of her.

Over the following months Betsy and her husband tried to resolve their differences, but while Betsy had become strong enough to withstand her parents' criticism, she was not able or willing to make amends with Steve. Having molded her into an image that satisfied him, he simply could not see why she needed to change, nor was he willing to compromise his lifestyle for her sake. Ultimately it came down to a choice between the marriage and Betsy's new priorities. When the marriage lost, Betsy could see that the relationship had been little more than an illusion from the very beginning. As painful as the separation was, it was also necessary.

If your parents denied you the autonomy, love, and respect you needed during childhood, you may gravitate toward people who remind you of them or treat you as they did. You may also project your parents' character traits onto people in your life who are not at all like them. In both cases, you are subconsciously trying to recreate your parents symbolically to resolve your relationship with them. Unfortunately, instead of releasing you, your adult relationships may simply perpetuate the problem. You will keep searching for the person or the accomplishment that will at last permit you to believe in yourself, when in fact the only person who can give you that permission is you.

Before you can approach life on genuinely meaningful terms, you may need to undo much of your parental conditioning. This is not an easy task, because it means reaching deep within yourself and confronting the unknown. It means challenging the values and goals that have defined your identity to this point. And it means confronting feelings that may have been buried for years and breaking deeply ingrained habits. Shaking yourself up to this extent will naturally threaten your security. You may feel as though you are losing your identity before you begin to regain it. Ultimately, however, this process will enable you to separate the dreams and beliefs that are truly yours from the prototype your family has imposed on you.

▼

CHART YOUR SUCCESS MILESTONES

How strong is your success habit? To find out whether your achievement pace is moving ahead of your achievement capacity, complete the following steps.

1. Create a time line by listing each year since you graduated from school. Then, moving across the page, make three more columns, with headings as follows:

| Year | Success Milestone | Life Choice | Setback |

2. In the second column, list all your success milestones beside the years in which they occurred.

Job change	Professional award
Salary increase	Honorary appointment
Promotion	Career change

3. In the third column, list all significant life choices beside the years in which they took place.

Marriage	Major vacation
Birth of a child	Child in private school/college
Move to a new home	
Purchase of a new home	New hobby (sports, collect-
Major acquisitions (car, pool,	ing, etc.)
art, home remodeling, etc.)	

4. In the fourth column, list all major setbacks beside the years in which they occurred.

Demotion	Forced relocation
Termination	Physical/emotional disability
Salary cut	Family/marital crisis
Strike/labor dispute	Financial distress

5. Examine the three sets to see how they relate to one another. Does the momentum build from one success to another? Does the pace of your acquisitions and other major life

choices increase as your successes build? Does the pattern of setbacks change as you move from milestone to milestone?

6. Using the patterns you've just discovered as a guide, try to chart the rest of your life. Do you expect your success momentum to keep increasing, or does it seem to be tapering off? What will happen in your personal life if you continue to experience the same sorts of milestones and setbacks?

7. Surveying the patterns of the past and your predictions of the future, do you feel that your pace allows you the time you need to savor your successes and learn from your mistakes? Do you derive enough satisfaction from the events and choices in the second and third columns to safely outweigh the setbacks in the fourth column? If your chart shows a constant increase in momentum in any or all areas, you may need to slow down, revise your game plan, and reevaluate which of your ambitions really matter.

7

▼

SUCCESS AND THE GENDER GAP

Woman is the victim of no mysterious fatality; the peculiarities that identify her as specifically a woman get their importance from the significance placed upon them.

— *Simone de Beauvoir*
The Second Sex

THE LITTLE GIRL was enchanting. She wore a long cotton print dress, white tights, and black patent leather Mary Janes. Her dark hair was tied with an impeccable bow. She sat quietly, her hands neatly folded in her lap, waiting for our session to begin. Only her lack of expression broke the spell. Like a china doll, she looked as though her face would crack if she dared to smile — or cry.

Her name was Maria — pronounced Ma-*rye*-ah, her mother carefully explained. Just six years old, she spoke French and Spanish, played piano, and read at a fourth-grade level. In most respects she was a model of achievement and grace. Yet her school had recommended therapy because she was not func-

158

tioning socially. Looking at her beautiful but inscrutable little face, I suspected that her social difficulties were only part of the story.

Maria's mother, Lorraine, had the same dark good looks as her daughter. Pencil thin, smartly coiffed, and dressed for success, she looked every inch the corporate vice president she was. When I asked to speak with Maria alone for a few minutes, Lorraine immediately asked if there was a phone outside from which she could make some business calls.

My initial consultation with Maria confirmed my suspicions that the whole family needed counseling. Unfortunately, the father, a senior executive with a major oil company, had recently divorced Lorraine and moved overseas with his new girlfriend. He was neither available nor willing to participate. Lorraine was not very cooperative either. Not that she wasn't concerned, she emphasized, she just didn't have the time. As it was, she was able to spend only about fifteen minutes of quality time with Maria a day. She would try to rearrange her schedule, but she couldn't guarantee anything.

It didn't take much insight to realize that Maria's social problems had developed because she was deeply unhappy at home. She felt rejected by her father and neglected by her mother. Her impressive academic and musical achievements represented a heartbreaking attempt to win their attention and affection, which earned her proud praise in the company of strangers but little more than a peck on the cheek at home. What Maria noticed most was her mother's constant clock-watching, which made the girl feel as if every moment they spent together was time stolen from her mother's other, more important life at work.

As rapidly as possible, I shifted the focus from Maria to Lorraine. At least if Maria felt she could count on the support and love of one parent, she would have a chance of developing the necessary emotional balance. But to deliver that security, Lorraine would have to do some serious soul-searching and make some critical changes in her life.

We began haltingly. Lorraine scheduled her sessions as early or late in the day as possible, wedging them between her many other commitments, but even so she frequently canceled at the last minute. I soon learned that her crowded calendar included not only her standing dates with Maria and her business appointments but also daily eight-mile runs. "If I don't do at least fifty miles a week I'm dysfunctional," she quipped. "Running is my real therapy."

"And if you don't keep setting and meeting similar goals in the rest of your life, you feel like a failure," I said, pushing her to confront the truth behind her compulsive schedule.

She looked at me suspiciously, resisting the inference. "If I don't set goals, I don't feel like a failure, but I don't move ahead as fast either. For example, if I hadn't pushed myself to my current running pace, I wouldn't be able to keep up with the men I run with from work, and I would have forfeited the respect and acceptance that I've gained by proving myself in their league. I also would be left out of the inside track of information about company deals and reshufflings. You'd be amazed what gets talked about during our runs!"

"You may be scoring some points for your career, but isn't it possible that your dedication to running is a signal of denial? Maybe you don't just want to run with those men, you want to become one of them. And to achieve *that* goal, you may be denying some of your roles as a woman."

Lorraine's response was so defensive that I knew I had hit a sensitive nerve. "Men make the rules in the business world. I don't have any choice but to accept their terms if I expect to get anywhere! And just proving that I'm equal is not enough; I've got to prove that I'm savvier, more aggressive, and more determined. I have to beat them at their own game."

The anger in Lorraine's voice was directed not at me but at

the many men who had dominated her life, beginning with her father, who had walked out on the family when she was twelve. Lorraine had watched her mother, a housewife with a high school education, struggle to support four children, first as a receptionist, then as a grocery store checker, and finally as a department store clerk. Lorraine had vowed that she would never allow herself to get caught in the trap of "female jobs," and by high school she'd gone into high gear in all the classes dominated by boys, including history, calculus, and physics. She won a scholarship to Yale, where she became manager of the men's lacrosse team before graduating Phi Beta Kappa with a combined major of Japanese and economics. Then, in rapid succession, she continued at Harvard Business School, married one of her classmates, and began working for a large textile firm.

"Were you also competitive with your husband?" I asked.

"We both thrived on competition, at least at first." Lorraine shifted uneasily in her seat. "We had very similar goals, and we'd race to see who advanced faster. I always viewed that as a plus because it motivated me, and beneath it all I assumed we were really rooting for each other." Abruptly she looked away, her jaw clenched and tears welling up in her eyes.

"He didn't feel the same way?"

She shook her head and briskly wiped away the tears. "Apparently not. I suppose I should have seen the signs when he accepted a job halfway across the country, just assuming that I'd follow him. I didn't challenge that because I actually landed a better job here, and the move ended up benefiting both our careers. I was so blind! He never wanted me to succeed at all. You know what he left me for? His secretary! Twenty years old, no education — no competition *there*. I guess that's what he wanted all along, and I never had a clue."

"Would you have played the part if you'd realized that's what he wanted?"

Her eyes went steely. "I'd sooner have died."

"You're very bitter because he walked out on you — just the way your father walked out on your mother. But what if he'd offered you a compromise? Let's say hypothetically that he told you he was having a difficult time at work and needed more support, or that he was concerned Maria needed more attention. Would you have cut back for the family's sake?"

"Why would it have to be me?" Lorraine retorted angrily, sidestepping the question. "Why is it always the woman who's asked to sacrifice everything for the family?"

"It's not always the woman," I replied. "I know a number of men who've taken years off from work so their wives could establish their careers. That's beside the point, though. I'm asking about you as a person, not as a man or a woman. Is your career more important to you than marriage or your daughter?"

The question stopped Lorraine cold. She sat stunned for several moments before attempting a response. "I watched my mother get swallowed up by marriage and motherhood, and I'm not willing to sacrifice myself that way. Maybe I am just selfish, but work gives me something tangible in return for my effort. The money, the praise, the promotions, all make me feel that I am worth something."

"And without all those strokes, you would feel like nothing," I said, completing the thought. She nodded almost imperceptibly. "What do you feel like when you're with Maria?"

"Ah, now the guilt trip," she said, taking a deep breath. "You want me to say that Maria means more to me than anything on earth, and I'd throw myself in front of a train for her —"

"I don't want you to say anything that you don't really feel," I said, interrupting her. "Loving someone doesn't have to involve killing yourself."

The admonishment seemed to unleash something deep within Lorraine, and she began to sob uncontrollably, as if letting out years of pent-up anguish.

"The truth is, I *do* love Maria that much," she confessed after several minutes, when the weeping had subsided. "But it's as though I'm carrying around this specter of motherhood. If I let myself care too much, I'm afraid I'll fall into some deep hole and never climb out. I'm afraid I'll lose myself in her, in that web of commitment."

"Isn't it possible that you're losing yourself in your work and your running instead? Why are you threatened by the idea of supporting your family when, at work, you're supporting something even more external — the company?"

"Why, I suppose because it gives me a sense of security and independent strength."

"Couldn't it also be that in trying to prove yourself among men, you've bought into some of their most self-destructive values? Aggressive competitiveness. Blind ambition. Material gains and advancement even at the expense of human relationships. Putting career demands ahead of family needs. And most dangerous of all, you seem to have fallen into the typically male trap of defining yourself by your job and how outsiders view you instead of relying on your own standards."

Lorraine stared at me, amazed. "I guess because I've always associated the traditional feminine values with weakness and dependence, I've never dared question male values. But maybe there are costs and benefits on both sides."

"If you're willing to develop a truly meaningful definition of success for yourself," I said, "you can achieve the balance between your relationship with Maria and your career that you both seem to need. But right now, you're heading for a serious crisis. Your external ambitions and your internal needs are colliding. And Maria is trapped in the middle."

Lorraine had her work cut out for her. She had to work through the aftereffects of her father's and then her husband's desertion, her mother's martyrdom, and her own blind acceptance of male success standards. Only after she had dispelled her shame and anxiety about being a woman would the pieces come together in a unified whole, allowing her to provide her daughter with the strong, confident, and loving role model the little girl so desperately needed. Only then could Lorraine assert herself at work without feeling she had to play catch-up with the men.

As any working woman knows, it's not easy to juggle the conflicting responsibilities of career, marriage, and motherhood. But the task is particularly difficult if you assume that the only way to succeed in business is to mimic male stereotypes and restrain your female side. While men have been the predominant force in American business for so long that they are deeply entrenched in their ways, women have a golden opportunity to revitalize and humanize the working world. Unfortunately, they have few role models to guide them. Most professional women, like most men, accept even the harshest of male standards without really questioning them. The challenge now facing women is to create their own brands of success, ideally blending the best of the traditional male and female values. The women who master this task will stand as role models for tomorrow's women *and* men.

Most of the advice that will help you establish a strong sense of inner success is contained in the other chapters of this book. It is not specific to women. Even in this chapter, the issues we examine apply primarily, but not exclusively, to women. Both sexes need to find new ways to integrate domestic and professional priorities. Both sexes need to reexamine the cultural influences that push them into stereotypical behavior patterns. And both sexes need to work together toward a more humane and equal society. While I can't do full justice to these themes in the space of just one chapter, I will try to penetrate the differences between men's and women's perceptions of success and suggest ways for all of us to learn from one another.

The Great Balancing Act

In 1973 less than 9 percent of college freshman women thought that "women's activities are best confined to the home and family" (down from 37 percent in 1970); of these, fewer than one in five expected to remain a housewife after her children were grown.[1] As of 1987, more than half of all adult American women were in the labor force, and 60 percent of working women were married.[2] But while men routinely place their professional identities ahead of their roles as husband and father, women who put their careers first often feel compelled to forgo marriage and motherhood rather than endure the emotional polarization caused by the contrasting roles.[3]

One reason for their emotional polarization is that many women simply don't believe they can succeed simultaneously on both fronts. Women are still generally expected to do the bulk of the work at home, whether or not they have outside jobs. This holds true throughout the world, including countries like the USSR, Norway, and China, where the vast majority of women work outside the home. Even if husband and wife clock the same number of hours on the job, the housework and child care remain primarily the wife's responsibility. To succeed across the board, then, the employed woman must work considerably harder than her husband.

Apart from their greater investment of labor in the home, women tend to be more interested in issues relating to home and family. Numerous studies dating back to 1931 have shown women to be more sensitive to family and other relationships, including social problems and cultural issues. They are more aware of aesthetics — the look and form of their surroundings, the sensory appeal of food, clothing, decor, and their own physical fitness. And they are more interested in religious and spiritual questions such as the intrinsic meaning of life. Even when women who had excelled in male-dominated professions like physics and medicine were compared with their male counterparts in the 1960s and 1970s, these disparities persisted. On personality tests, these women appeared to be more responsible, more highly socialized, more tolerant, more cooperative, and more alert to moral and ethical issues.[4]

The values that apparently motivate women in their work are also very different from the ones that typically drive men. In their study of female corporate managers, Margaret Hennig and Anne Jardim concluded that "women see a career as personal growth, as self-fulfillment, as satisfaction, as making a contribution to others, as doing what one wants to do. While men indubitably want these things, too, when they visualize a career they see it as a series of jobs, a progression of jobs, as a path leading upward, with concrete recognition and reward implied."[5]

Men generally show more interest in critical thinking and objective problem solving. They are more concerned with economic or utilitarian issues than aesthetic or social ones. And they tend to value personal power, influence, and fame more than women do.[6] Men's primary concerns all fit neatly within the parameters of the working world that they have shaped, but they also tend to hold men back from the more balanced life experience that generates internal success. As a result, men are more prone to mid-life crises, heart attacks, alcoholism, and drug abuse, and they have a shorter life expectancy. For all the obstacles facing women in the business world, their basic values give them a real advantage in life.

Competing at Work

Despite the rising numbers of women in the work force and far-reaching equal opportunity legislation, women's career opportunities are still far from equal to men's. Most women are subtly encouraged to take positions offering lower pay and prestige than those offered to men with comparable qualifications, and just as frequently are discouraged — or actively prevented — from seeking posts in which they could accumulate power, respect, and wealth. The result of this conditioning is evident in the ratio of men to women in jobs that involve similar skills but disparate levels of prestige and salary. Among health workers, for example, only 15 percent of doctors and other health diagnosing professionals were women as of 1986, but more than 85 percent of "health assessment and treating" professionals, such as nurses and technicians, were female. At the same time, in the academic world, women constituted more than 73 percent of all teachers below college level but only 36 percent of college and university professors. While 83 percent of all elementary school teachers were women, 81 percent of school principals were men. And in the business world, male executives outnumbered women executives by almost two to one, but female administrative support and clerical workers outnumbered their male counterparts by almost *four* to one.[7] Despite the annual addition of more than one million women to the labor force each year, the ratios of women to men in high-echelon jobs have not significantly changed in the past decade. Women across the board are still paid approximately one-third less than men for work of comparable worth, though a 1987 report on corporate America showed that women at the vice-presidential level and above earned 42 percent less than their male peers.[8] Even in this age of equal opportunity, the higher the prestige and power attached to a given job, the higher the probability that the job is held by a man. In 1988 only one percent of the top five hundred corporate chiefs in America were female.

Women who buck the status quo and pursue a leadership role are expected not just to conform to the white male prototype within that specialty but to surpass men at their own game.

Surveys of top executives indicate that for women to climb the corporate ladder, they must prove themselves tough and independent, but also depend on others. They must prove themselves more competent than men, and in a wider variety of skills, yet they're expected to appear and sound feminine. While they're supposed to give their jobs top priority, they must accept lower positions and salaries than their male equals.[9] The wage discrepancy holds even for female Harvard MBA graduates, though the inequity may lie in the bonus system or perks rather than actual salary.

The double standard has become so engrained that women tend to undervalue their own performance. When boys and girls are asked to complete a task and then reward themselves with candy, girls typically "pay" themselves less than boys do, a pattern that persists into adulthood. When assigned a job and then asked to rank their performance and give themselves the reward they deserve, women consistently give themselves less than they've earned, while men take the rewards justified by their performance.[10] However, women evaluate their performance accurately when using criteria other than material rewards. Either they don't equate external compensation with success, or they've been conditioned by our culture to expect unequal payment.[11]

When judged by more objective standards, of course, neither sex is intellectually superior to the other.[12] SAT and IQ tests show that boys generally do less well on verbal and better on spatial and mechanical questions (a reflection of the typical male bias toward things and theories rather than communication and human interrelation), but overall scores are equivalent. In school, girls generally get better marks and skip grades more frequently than boys.

Yet many girls begin to pull back from direct competition with boys as they enter adolescence. Suddenly they begin grooming themselves to step into the roles their mothers and older sisters have modeled for them, which until very recently excluded most positions of leadership. Also, teenage girls for the first time must contend with boys as sexual partners and future husbands as well as classmates. Many cannot reconcile the notions of competition and love. "If I'm out there trying to whip his ass on the tennis court or in the classroom," explained one of my sixteen-year-old patients, "he's never going to ask me out. If I *beat* him, he'll never speak to me again." Achievement and desirability appear to be mutually exclusive, as if achievement is unfeminine.[13] Opting for desirability, many adolescent girls show a drop in academic performance just at the time when most boys begin to buckle down.

Fortunately, not all girls succumb to this pattern. Those who are actively discouraged from viewing themselves as inferior and instead are urged to explore and develop independently and observe a wide variety of male and female role models often pursue diverse goals, even in male-dominated professions. Top women executives and professionals generally come from families that encouraged and supported their education and achievement without pressuring them to conform to "feminine" stereotypes. The vast majority of these women were only or eldest children or had no brothers.[14] In a sample of women presidents and vice presidents of the country's major corporations in 1973, *all* were firstborns and none had brothers.[15]

These patterns beg the question, Do girls achieve more when separated from boys? Curiously, while many bastions of male education, like Harvard and Yale, have bowed to feminist pressure and gone coed, researchers have found that this may actually be a disservice to the incoming women. Men generally work harder and persist longer under the scrutiny of other men, but women are more motivated to excel apart from men. While most male-dominated schools encourage the same toughness and competitiveness that prevail in business, all-women colleges generally have a more cooperative and supportive atmosphere, which tends to foster leadership abilities and motivate students to seek a higher degree of personal accomplishment. Finally, because the ratio of women's faculty to students is greater, students are exposed to more diverse female role models.

One study found that the more women there were on the faculty of a given college, the more of that college's women graduates went on to earn Ph.D.'s and a place in *Who's Who of American Women*.[16] Women's school graduates seem to emerge from the confusion of adolescence with a stronger sense of their own competence and are generally less intimidated by men than women who attended school alongside men. They also may be more willing to rely on other women in their professions, building alliances and support networks instead of competing with one another for the attention of male superiors.

Such alliances are a vital source of strength and could help women reverse the inequities of the business world. Not that women should start defining themselves by their salary in the way that many men do, but until they receive fair compensation, women will remain economically subservient. As long as women are paid like second-class citizens, they will undoubtedly be treated like second-class citizens, which will inhibit their financial and emotional independence and drive them right back into subservience. Breaking the pattern of undercompensation will not lure more women into becoming ersatz men; it will help free them to enter careers of their own choosing.

One way to achieve equal pay and independence, of course, is to become the boss, and more and more women are realizing this. According to the U.S. Small Business Administration, women already own one-third of the nation's businesses and are starting new ones at twice the rate of men. Moreover, the SBA estimates that the survival rate for female-owned businesses is about 20 to 30 percent higher than that of male-owned businesses, possibly because women tend to be more cautious than men about risk taking.[17]

The more women use money and power to further their own

causes and concerns, the less likely they will be to fall into the typical male pattern of pursuing material rewards as ends unto themselves. In this way economic equality can give women the security and clout to pursue more far-reaching change, possibly increasing the level of social responsibility and human sensitivity in business and in the world at large.

Competing with Family and Friends

Women are by no means immune to the competitive urge, but they rarely compete as directly and openly as men do, and their contests are often a cover for frustration or anxiety. If you don't work outside the home, for example, but most of your friends and acquaintances do, you may feel obliged to justify your career choice by turning homemaking and child rearing into a competitive occupation. Instead of battling for raises and promotions, you may find yourself subtly, perhaps even unconsciously, vying for social rank based on the behavior and academic performance of your children, your visibility in school and community affairs, and the decor of your home.

If you do have an outside career, you may engage in similar competitions, but the impulse may be connected more with guilt or habit than with defensiveness. Parents naturally want to give their children the best, but as a working parent your impulse may be to give your child a little extra — more and better clothes or toys, more special lessons, more exposure to museums and the arts — to compensate for the time you are away from home. If you see another child with greater material advantages, you may hasten to bring yours up to par. And if your child misbehaves or underperforms in one of her special classes, you may interpret her "failure" as your own. You throw yourself into the task of boosting her achievements, because as long as she's surpassing the others in her age group, you can reassure yourself that it's okay to have your own career. Though you probably don't consciously realize it, your child's external accomplishments have become a condition of your own external success.

However, the guilt that you may feel as a working mother could be misplaced. Most children benefit from seeing their mothers in roles of responsibility and authority outside the home.[18] It tends to make them more respectful of women in general and more open-minded about the kinds of jobs women can perform. In many dual-career families, children receive more attention from their fathers than they would if their mothers were homemakers.

Rather than allowing yourself to feel guilty about working or defensive about not working, you may do better to consider what your *child* needs to feel successful. Parents' most well-intentioned efforts to inspire achievement in their children often have unwelcome consequences. The children may

▼ experience stress as a result of complicated scheduling.
▼ feel pressured to perform well.
▼ have little time to relax and act like children.
▼ develop the attitude that playing is unimportant, something to do with leftover time and energy.
▼ overvalue or undervalue money and status.
▼ feel that their parents won't love or approve of them unless they are high achievers.

High achievement won't make your child feel secure or happy if, in the push to achieve, she loses her intrinsic motivation. Without the opportunity and encouragement to play, relax, or daydream, she may strive to please you without adequately developing her own interests. This is how the quest for external validation and the suppression of internal success cycle from one generation to the next.

Conflicts over success can occur in your marriage, too, with varying consequences. If you and your partner are independently pushing for more pay, higher title, more power or visibility outside the home, there are apt to be some related adjustments within the family. How this will affect the balance of power at home is not always easy to predict. Many husbands who espouse egalitarianism in theory complain that their wives' careers actually produce a net loss for the family by increasing the tax rate and the amount spent on clothes, transportation, and household help and reducing the amount of time available for the marriage and children. By the same token, many men who oppose the idea of women working in general find that when *their* wives work, the children become more responsible, their wives seem more interesting, and the family's cash flow problems are reduced. With husbands as with all of us, there's not always a direct correlation between expectation and reality.

Most women benefit emotionally from working, especially if their jobs accommodate marital and parental responsibilities and they have their husbands' support. A professional career inspires a much different sense of confidence, competence, and intellectual involvement from that of a domestic career, though each may be satisfying in its own way. Women benefit greatly from both types of career, and most women now feel that they can manage to have both, though not always at the same time.

Having both becomes difficult, however, if you have a highly competitive marriage. If you are vying with each other for professional rank and income, you can't possibly share in each other's success. In fact, as John and Candice of Chapter 2 proved, the more outside recognition either of you receives, the more your marriage will suffer. The alternative is to respect each other's goals and work together to manage the practical complications of a two-career marriage. By supporting each other, you become part of each other's success.

Sometimes, though, women carry supportiveness to extremes and run the risk of losing themselves in the process. Many political and celebrity wives fall into this category, funneling their own social and financial ambitions into their husband's careers. The assumption is that they will gain status and power through their husbands' achievements, yet many of these women ultimately end up competing for attention with the very careers they helped to build!

One of my patients, who is married to a television producer, complained that she rarely sees her husband more than two or three hours a day, and during active production he is often away on location for up to two months at a stretch. "He says he has no choice because it's the nature of the business," she told me, "but I feel as if I have to fight for his attention even when he's home. I know he loves his work — and I certainly benefit from his success — but sometimes I think he cares more about his work than me." Such women are caught in the double bind of enjoying the material benefits of their husbands' professional status while resenting its high emotional toll on their marriage and family life. They face a tough choice between status and love.

Why Should a Woman Be More Like a Man?

"It's a man's world," the saying goes, and you may feel that if you don't operate like a man you'll never gain equal standing. But in your haste to move ahead, you may be overlooking the dark side of the male world. The most significant and disturbing difference between the sexes is that men in our culture frequently are actively motivated to dominate, even to the point of hurting other people. While most women show a distinct desire for interpersonal harmony and an aversion to conflict, many men relish physical, intellectual, and financial combat. This, no doubt, accounts for the statistics that nine out of ten violent crimes are committed by men and that virtually all the players in Wall Street's increasingly ruthless game of hostile corporate takeovers are men.

But are males inherently more aggressive and offensively competitive, or does our culture condition them to fit this mold? In a survey of teenagers in ten industrialized nations, researchers found that men consistently are associated with power and women with relationships and emotions. The behavior and values of the youths themselves reflected this split, with boys consistently measuring higher in self-centeredness and self-indulgence, while girls measured higher in other-orientedness and emotional openness.[19]

Yet Margaret Mead's cross-cultural comparisons show that children who are raised in nonindustrialized, tribal settings do not necessarily conform to these patterns. In New Guinea she found two contrasting groups that denied such sex differences almost entirely, instead conditioning all youngsters to adopt "unisex" personality traits. In the mountain tribe known as the Arapesh, everyone was expected to be loving, caring, and nurturing. Aggressiveness was discouraged and cooperation praised. As a result, boys and girls were equally nurturant, and the tribe experienced almost no murder or violence, except as a defense against outsiders.

If the Arapesh were able to "feminize" their boys, the headhunters known as the Mundugumor succeeded equally well in endowing their daughters with "masculine" traits. This tribe taught aggression and punished nurturant behavior. Even in sex, kisses and caresses were out; foreplay consisted of scratching and biting. As a result, both sexes displayed an abundance of hostility, hatred, suspicion, and competitiveness.[20] The Mundugumor represent a cautionary example for American women who feel they can gain only by emulating men. The Arapesh, on the other hand, represent a heartening example of how society might change if women took a more active stand in asserting not only their rights but their values as well.

In our society, men are more accepted in the workplace than women and therefore command better pay and more prestige, but they are also pressured to define themselves primarily by such external milestones as title, salary, and achievement awards. Concentration on career tends to undercut other vital sources of fulfillment, such as hobbies, friends, volunteer activities, and, all too often, marriage and family. The rare man who voluntarily chooses to quit a good job or work part-time in order to spend more time with his children is still viewed as an oddity and a loser by the majority of our society. He's expected to put career ahead of family without ever questioning which is more important to him personally. To conform to this cultural model, men sacrifice just as much personal gratification as women gain from their multiple roles.

These roles offer women other advantages as well. If you function as mother, wife, housekeeper, cook, and hostess outside the office, you are less prone to be pulled into the group persona of your career specialty. The relationships and interests you cultivate in your private life can also provide backup support, solace, and welcome distraction when, as occasionally happens to almost everyone, male or female, your career falters.

Even when you take on the same jobs as men, you do not necessarily have to perform them "like a man." Anyone who wants to advance professionally must demonstrate some of the same general traits: firmness, decisiveness, competence, assertiveness, confidence, and ability to calculate risks. But these are all value-neutral traits, and it's by asserting your values that you can gain your true advantage as a woman and as an individual. How you apply this advice to yourself, of course, will depend on your particular goals and priorities. However, many of the same qualities that make you an appealing person, a responsible spouse, and an effective parent can also make you a strong and effective leader at work. A good manager must be sensitive to human relationships and responsive to emotional conflicts. An effective executive inspires cooperation and trust and encourages the free exchange of ideas. This is all true for men too, of course, but men tend to display their sensitivity and responsiveness in a more restrained manner. In many instances, your feminine warmth, empathy, tolerance, and sensitivity can be definite assets.

Aside from the personal benefits you stand to gain by asserting yourself as a woman, you can help to change society for the better. Sexual equality is not just a women's issue. Both men and women have been restricted for too long by traditional stereotypes and sex roles. Once these barriers are at last overcome, men and women will find that both sides have a great deal to learn from each other. "If we once accept the premise that we can build a better world by using the different gifts of each sex," wrote Margaret Mead, "we shall have two kinds of freedom, freedom to use untapped gifts of each sex, and freedom to admit freely and cultivate in each sex their special superiorities."[21]

▼

CHOOSING THE RIGHT CAREER: A PLAN

The following guidelines, which are only slightly more applicable to women than to men, will help you put your personal values to work for you on the job.

A. Choosing an occupation

1. Assess the profiles of women in the profession you're considering. Do you consider them positive role models? If the profession is highly dominated by men, decide whether you are prepared to be a pioneer and whether the intrinsic rewards of the job are enough to outweigh the risk of discrimination.
2. Consider the nature of competitiveness in this occupation. Would you be forced to compete with other women, or with both men and women? Are you comfortable with the level of competitiveness?
3. Consider your priorities at home: family, marriage, social life, educational goals. How will the balance of your time and energy be affected by this potential career change? If your job demands too great a sacrifice at home, look for ways to reformat it: working at home part-time, sharing your responsibilities with a coworker, or reorganizing your schedule. Also look for ways to lighten your load at home: arranging cooperative child care with another family, hiring household help, or assigning some of your responsibilities to other family members.
4. How much money do you need to make? Will the job you're contemplating satisfy your financial needs?
5. Weigh your personal skills and interests. Will this job be challenging enough to hold you? Does it afford enough opportunities for growth and development for women as well as men?

B. Managing relationships

1. Rely on your relationships as a personal and professional resource. Don't be afraid to cultivate friendships at work or to lean on your family for emotional support.

2. Assert yourself as a woman without apology. Be open, honest, and confident in dealing with others.
3. Utilize the same skills that help you build relationships with friends and family members to develop your relationships with coworkers.
4. Recognize the balance between individual merit and politics that exists in most professions. As personally rewarding as excellence may be, it is rarely the sole criterion for advancement. You can cultivate your political savvy through relationship building without compromising your idealism. However, if you find that your senses of quality and integrity are at risk, you may need to reconsider the direction of your career.

C. *Managing money*

1. Prove your competence, then demand a price that's fair. If necessary, research what men are paid for similar services.
2. Be prepared to turn down unfair offers. Only if *you* believe that your work is worth the going rate will you be able to persuade others that it is.
3. Use what you earn to leverage future choices. Your ultimate goal is not just to make more money but to lead a more satisfying life. Invest in causes and pursuits that bring you true gratification.

D. *Managing power*

1. Trust your inner resources and resist outside attempts to intimidate or discriminate against you.
2. Learn to differentiate between objective criticism, discrimination, and personal attacks. The better you understand the other person's motivation, the more effective and appropriate your response is likely to be. Many women make a mistake in interpreting every negative

remark as a personal assault. This causes unnecessary emotional trauma and prevents them from learning from constructive criticism.

3. Channel your emotional responses into constructive activity. Instead of turning your anger and frustration against yourself, your family, or the people around you, use that energy to develop new opportunities.

4. Draw on your ability to read people in relationships to develop insights into the people with whom you work. Use these insights to engender support for your ideas and causes.

5. Don't allow yourself to get so caught up in your own career that you lose your concern for others. Having a strong social conscience and a strong sense of family are vital sources of power for women and men. Women stand to lose more than they gain if they sacrifice these strengths in the pursuit of superficial equality.

▼

YOUR SEX ROLE INVENTORY

To find out how your perceptions of sex roles have evolved and how they may be affecting your feelings about yourself, complete the following steps.

1. To the right of each characteristic below, make a check mark in the appropriate column(s) if (a) you identify it with yourself, (b) you ideally would like it to describe you, (c) you identify it with your mother, (d) you identify it with your father, or (e) you identify it as traditionally male or female.

Characteristic	Self	Ideal self	Mother	Father	Male/ female
Intelligent	—	—	—	—	—
Creative	—	—	—	—	—
Ambitious	—	—	—	—	—
Attractive	—	—	—	—	—
Nurturing	—	—	—	—	—
Aggressive	—	—	—	—	—
Powerful	—	—	—	—	—
Persistent	—	—	—	—	—
Competitive	—	—	—	—	—
Cooperative	—	—	—	—	—
Perceptive	—	—	—	—	—
Judgmental	—	—	—	—	—
Petty	—	—	—	—	—
Dishonest	—	—	—	—	—
Combative	—	—	—	—	—
Empathetic	—	—	—	—	—
Sensitive	—	—	—	—	—
Serious	—	—	—	—	—
Moralistic	—	—	—	—	—
Tolerant	—	—	—	—	—
Patient	—	—	—	—	—
Compassionate	—	—	—	—	—
Seductive	—	—	—	—	—

▼

YOUR SEX ROLE INVENTORY

Characteristic	Self	Ideal self	Mother	Father	Male/ female
Secure	—	—	—	—	—
Competent	—	—	—	—	—
Honest	—	—	—	—	—
Assertive	—	—	—	—	—
Inquisitive	—	—	—	—	—
Analytic	—	—	—	—	—
Charismatic	—	—	—	—	—
Catty	—	—	—	—	—
Altruistic	—	—	—	—	—
Selfish	—	—	—	—	—
Sincere	—	—	—	—	—

2. Compare the traits you identify with yourself and those you ideally would like to describe you. If these two lists differ significantly, you may be setting ideals for yourself that are too far out of reach. The results could be anxiety, frustration, discontent, and a feeling of failure. Instead of striving to become something you are not, you may need to reevaluate your ideals.

3. Check to see how your own attributes compare with those of your parents. If yours skew heavily in favor of one parent over the other, it indicates that you may not have learned all you could from both sides. It may also mean that you are adopting that parent's roles without permitting yourself alternatives. Remember that parental conditioning does not have to be a life sentence; as an adult, you owe it to yourself to select only the roles that suit your individual values and priorities.

4. How many of your personal traits do you consider to be traditionally male? How many female? If your list skews heavily toward one sex over the other, you may be overly influenced by sexual stereotypes.

182

PART IV

TOWARD A NEW PHILOSOPHY OF SUCCESS

8

▼

FOR LOVE *and* MONEY:
TOWARD A NEW
DEFINITION OF SUCCESS

If I am what I have and if what I have is lost, who then am I?

— *Erich Fromm*

ONE OF THE reasons external success is so compelling is that it promises so much. In a period of rising inflation and imminent recession, money offers the illusion of security. When Nancy Reagan's $950 place settings become a standard for the "new elegance," opulence offers the illusion of chic. When power brokers like Donald Trump, Carl Icahn, and T. Boone Pickens are accorded the status of modern folk heros, it's not surprising that college freshmen rate "becoming wealthy" as more important than developing a "meaningful philosophy of life."[1] It takes imagination, self-knowledge, and courage to resist such a strong cultural tide of materialism. You need to know what you really want, what will make you happy, and what matters to you personally. For what appears obvious about success — that it brings unlimited pleasure — is largely illusion. And what seems illusory — that we all can attain it — is its real substance.

To understand how this can be, you have to look past the superficial trappings that are supposed to denote success and examine the actual dynamics of personal gratification.

The Requirements of Success

The following table presents some of the most pervasive myths about what's necessary to *achieve* success today alongside what you actually need to *be* successful, to integrate a satisfying personal life with fulfilling professional pursuits. The message is not necessarily that all the items in the first column are harmful to your health or career, only that they do not constitute the secret of success. Depending on your particular activities and interactions, you may have to draw from this list on occasion. But if your main goal is to achieve enduring personal satisfaction, concentrate primarily on developing the resources in the second column.

TRUE SUCCESS REQUIRES . . .

Myth	Reality
1. Narrow focus/singular goal	Diverse roles/multiple goals
2. Self-promotion	Self-trust and self-expression
3. Independence	Interdependence
4. Manipulation	Honesty
5. Perfection	Growth
6. High stress	Physical and emotional fitness
7. Sheer willpower	The ability to recognize and capitalize on good luck
8. Absolute consistency	Flexibility
9. Systematic thinking	Creative thinking
10. Pragmatism	Idealism

Let's examine these myths and realities one by one, beginning with some questions to help you clarify your own assumptions about success.

1. Narrow focus/singular goal versus diverse roles/multiple goals

Is your life oriented around one particular goal?
Do you make time for hobbies, interests, and friends outside work?
Are you postponing important personal decisions pending a major achievement at work?

Many of my patients characterize themselves as highly competitive, ambitious professionals and then, in the same breath, admit that they never have time or energy for the pursuits that give them real personal satisfaction. When I ask if their ambition gives them any satisfaction, many give a perplexed shrug. Competitive ambition does generate a certain heat and fervor that for many feel like pleasure but when this pleasure comes at the expense of deeply meaningful relationships, activities, and interests, the net effect is negative.

But, my patients protest, the only way to get ahead is by focusing on a single goal and going for it tooth and nail. Forget about *feeling* successful, they declare; you have to look at what it takes to *acquire* success. So be it. On both counts, it is counterproductive to have a narrow focus and a singular goal. Among the abundance of research that supports this position is the Grant study, mentioned in Chapter 1, which tracked a group of Harvard College graduates for more than fifty years. The participants who have had the most successful careers were not necessarily academic superstars in school, and their professional ambitions have not wholly defined their lives in the years since. Instead, they have allowed themselves to build strong, stable marriages and deep friendships. They have made room in their lives for exercise, relaxation, and multiple interests and activities. As a result, they have become best-selling authors, cabinet members, scholars, physicians, judges, and captains of industry. In short, they have shown an abundance of initiative rather than blinding ambition.[2] This distinction is important, because initiative tends to enliven and open us up to new ideas and opportunities, while ambition tends to enclose us.

This is not to say that ambition per se is dangerous, or that you should not have any goals. Viewed within the broad context of your life, ambition can be a strong motivator, and goals can help you organize your time and energy. The danger arises when you allow just one goal to define your life. Time and again my patients tell me that they must first reach a certain level of professional success before they can get married, have a child, take up a sport or hobby, or even spend time with a dear friend or relative. Their assumption is that if they push themselves hard enough and attach all these extra incentives to the effort, they can make their professional dream come true, after which all the other goals will come easily.

But in the first place, professional success is not always a direct function of ambition; luck, timing, skill, and longevity are often more potent factors. In the second place, personal deprivation actually makes it more difficult to concentrate on work and thus impedes professional advancement. You are more likely to succeed both personally and professionally if you embrace three key pursuits in different areas — for example, work, family life, and leisure activity — than if you focus entirely on a single objective.

In *The Conquest of Happiness*, Bertrand Russell wrote that the secret of happiness is to "let your interests be as wide as possible and let your reactions to the things and persons that interest you be as far as possible friendly rather than hostile." The more you open yourself up — to ideas, relationships, and activities — the more you will enjoy the process of living and the less your goals will limit you.

2. Self-promotion versus self-trust and self-expression

Do you strive to appear more successful to others than you
think you really are?
Do you fear being disliked?
Do you respect yourself?

The myth of self-promotion arises out of the commercialism
of society. We buy and sell products. We buy and sell services.
It's not really surprising that we've come to view ourselves as
commodities as well. There is a pervasive assumption that success depends on how well we "sell" ourselves. It's not enough
to be talented, skillful, and creatively involved in our work; we
have to round out the package with an engaging personality,
physical charm, and powerful connections. If we don't come by
the whole package naturally, we have to fake it. Erich Fromm,
describing self-promotion in terms of what he called the marketing character, wrote:

> The aim of the marketing character is complete adaptation, so
> as to be desirable under all conditions of the personality mar-
> ket. The marketing character personalities do not even *have*
> egos (as people in the nineteenth century did) to hold on to,
> that belong to them, that do not change. For they constantly
> change their egos, according to the principle: "I am as you
> desire me."[3]

Unfortunately, in the process of promoting ourselves, we often
confuse acceptance with self-respect. We want so badly for
everyone to like us that we may neglect those who love us the
most and make it almost impossible to love ourselves. Then,
when outsiders do not buy our promotional package, we feel
that we've failed. Our notion of success is so wrapped up in
appearances that it distorts our perspective and costs us our self-
worth.

All too often the concentration on a packaged image also
eclipses the development of the skill, talent, and creativity that

are required for real growth and advancement. As a result, the self-promoter can end up losing both psychologically and professionally when the employer/buyers begin to look for the substance inside that impressive package.

Meaningful success requires not self-promotion but self-trust. For in the end, the facade you mold and refine to someone else's specifications is far less important than your core identity, including your values, ideals, talents, and dreams. When you are committed to expressing your deeper self, it becomes very difficult to change, chameleonlike, to fit the latest marketing trends. Yet when you trust yourself, you exude the capability, pride, confidence, and conviction that make you impressive to others. Sure, there will be those who disagree with you, and not everyone will like you, but you will build strong, meaningful relationships with those who share your beliefs and outlook, and even among your rivals, you will command widespread respect for your integrity. That respect, supported by inner conviction, is what separates truly successful leaders from followers.

With self-trust comes self-acceptance, which means accepting *all* of yourself, including your full range of emotions. The emphasis on stoicism in our culture borders on desensitization. We routinely look away when walking past the homeless on our city streets. We stare dispassionately at television programs and films in which men, women, and children are subjected to torture and violence. We force ourselves to grin when we are desperately unhappy and to restrain ourselves when we are elated. In the business world, especially, decorum is an essential part of the standard veneer. But decorum can have a deadening effect on the core self, and if we have stifled our ability to feel, how can we ever know fulfillment?

The problem of feeling and expressing emotions affects men and women equally, but in different ways. For men, the challenge is to break through the conditioned defenses against feelings of pain, sadness, and fear. Men need to allow themselves to cry and ask for support, to show their humanness. For women, the challenge is to confront their anger. Women are allowed to cry when they are sad, but when they feel angry or oppressed, society says, "C'mon, honey. Let's see that pretty smile." In other words, put on a happy face, because your feelings don't really matter. Well, feelings do matter, and men and women alike need to take possession of *all* their emotions if we are to fully trust ourselves or one another.

3. Independence versus interdependence

> Are you active in groups, clubs, or associations?
> Do other people's problems concern you?
> Are you responsible to anyone but yourself?

"Look out for number one," the underlying motto of the "me" generation of fifties baby boomers, is one reason young adults are experiencing record rates of divorce, depression, and suicide. What began as a celebration of individuality has turned into a generational trend toward emotional isolation. Self-assertiveness has been confused with selfishness. Achievement has been confused with dominance. In this context, independence does not engender a positive feeling of success. It engenders anxiety, mistrust, alienation, and guilt, the emotional benchmarks of failure.

This fiercely defensive brand of independence even has a negative impact on career advancement, as one of my patients found out the hard way. An associate producer for a television news program, she became enraged when a less qualified producer was placed above her. Instead of approaching the producer directly, she confronted the show's executive producer with work samples that, she thought, would prove she deserved to have the job. To her face the executive producer was polite, but he said that this was a bureaucratic appointment and his hands were tied; perhaps she could work with the producer to help him get up to speed? The associate producer, bent on advancing her own career, could barely stand to speak to her competitor, much less help him! Yet she soon realized how much her selfishness was costing her when colleagues began to give her the cold shoulder. Had she helped the struggling producer, she would have proved herself a team player and earned the entire staff's respect. Instead, by treating her career as an independent venture instead of an interdependent process, she found herself suddenly locked out of the team and any immediate chance of advancement.

At the other end of the spectrum, people who go out of their way to help or serve others often enjoy surprisingly powerful benefits. In 1988 the Institute for the Advancement of Health in New York City conducted a survey of more than seventeen hundred women who regularly volunteer to help others. The participants reported that helping another person not only generates emotional satisfaction but has physical benefits as well, including increased energy and a "helper's calm" that can provide relief from stress-related disorders such as high blood pressure, headaches, and body aches and pains. The positive effects are not limited to the time spent actively helping, but can actually be revived just by remembering that time.[4]

Of course, most of us realize the greatest benefits of interdependence through family and other close personal relationships. Given stability, constancy, and love, these relationships can provide the vital support we need to weather the triumphs and tragedies of everyday life. In a world where individuals are categorized by their occupation and superficial appearance, and valued accordingly, these intimate attachments provide a deeper, more meaningful sense of belonging. Our family and friends cherish us not just for what we do or how we look, but for who we are and what we feel, for our uniqueness. We are responsible to them, and they to us. The resulting sense of connectedness is what makes us feel personally important and secure.

4. Manipulation versus honesty

> Are you willing to defend your beliefs publicly?
> Do you try to outmaneuver people who get in your way?
> Do you try to make others think that you agree with them even when you don't?

Some years ago, Michael Korda made the best-seller list with two books, *Power!* and *Success!*, which offered readers a host of tactical power plays designed to give them more clout in the office. His suggestions included the positioning of one's desk, the location of one's office, manipulative use of the telephone, as well as the same kind of personal appearance guidelines that are now known as dressing for success. Yet behind all the clever how-tos, the real message of these books was this: to succeed in your career, you have to manipulate others into feeling inferior to you while at the same time deceiving them into thinking you are much more valuable than you really are. Anyone who prefers to concentrate on the work at hand rather than the position of buttons on a sleeve or the color of a briefcase might as well forget about making it to the top.

This message has been echoed in scores of subsequent instructional guides, creating the widespread impression that legitimacy and honesty are detrimental to professional success. Two facts contradict this illusion. Number one, most people who achieve bona fide professional success — whether in business, politics, science, or the arts — are too busy with the substance of their work to pay much attention to the trivial details that consume most manipulators. Can you imagine Pablo Picasso trying to impress art collectors by positioning his easel in the power corner of his studio? Or Albert Schweitzer dressing for success?

The second argument against manipulation is that it breeds mistrust and resentment. Those who wangle their way into positions of authority rarely have the support of those around them and frequently must contend with open hostility from the ranks.

Sometimes these impasses lead to coup attempts and sometimes to lingering alienation; unless they are able to display genuine leadership ability, the manipulators usually experience professional and emotional defeat.

When you deal with the world honestly, you treat the people around you not as pawns but as partners. This involves much more than simply telling the truth. It means that you look at all sides of a situation before drawing up your game plan. It means being evenhanded — criticizing yourself but also defending your own rights, criticizing others but also defending *their* rights. Acting honestly means that you invest your personal values in everything you do instead of simply conforming to expected patterns of behavior. In all these ways, you let others know that you have respect for yourself and for them. And you earn their respect.

5. Perfection versus growth

Do you have to be the best to feel good about yourself?
Do you try to conceal and forget your mistakes?
Do you consider your work drudgery or play?

James Michener once said, "I like challenges. I don't mind defeat. I don't gloat over victories. I want to be in the ballgame."[5] The important idea here is that fulfillment involves a process of growth rather than the achievement of perfection, which is often equated with success.

Unfortunately, the myth of success as perfection runs throughout the business world, where constant victory is seen as a condition for progress. Few companies allow for the natural tidal motion of growth. Instead, achievers are expected to catapult from one triumph to the next, rising ever higher, never backtracking. But even the strongest performer eventually hits a time when the challenge is just too great. The logical reaction at this point is to backtrack to a position of strength, accept the situation, and regroup before attempting to move ahead again. The organization, unfortunately, may resist this strategy, treating the impasse instead as a failure for which the punishment is demotion — and humiliation. The performer who has consistently excelled is suddenly stopped cold and may never recover. The temporary setback that could have been a valuable learning opportunity instead becomes an insurmountable barrier to forward progress. Such shortsightedness imposes unnecessary losses on both the individual and the organization.

The moments when you attain a goal and realize true perfection probably account for less than 2 percent of your lifetime, while the process of living and working toward your goals occupies the rest. If you look to perfection to supply your sense of success, you are discounting the other 98 percent of your life — truly a self-defeating arrangement. But when you turn it around, making the process the real source of success, you give yourself permission to enjoy life as a whole, to accept and learn from your mistakes, and to take your achievements in stride. By incorporating a sense of success into everything you do, you enable yourself to grow in ways that are personally meaningful and rewarding.

By concentrating on process and discovery rather than perfection, you allow yourself to be playful both in your life and in your work. You open yourself to spontaneous thought and action as well as risk taking. You challenge the limitations of standard reasoning. You permit yourself to enjoy what you're doing and to let the momentum of your pleasure generate new insights and achievements.

Civilization's greatest geniuses, from Leonardo to Einstein, have all understood the value of play. The downfall of Americans, laboring under misinterpretation of both the Protestant work ethic and the meaning of success, is that we too often treat work as a penalty instead of a privilege, then look to leisure to compensate for an unsatisfying career. This makes it virtually impossible to achieve the kind of internal balance that true success requires. The solution is to revive playfulness in work as well as in leisure. Enthusiasm is a far more powerful motivator than desire or necessity, and as such is a more reliable source of success.

6. High stress versus physical and emotional fitness

Are you too busy to exercise?
Do you allow yourself time to do nothing each day?
Do you think it's worthwhile to put in fifteen-hour days and seven-day workweeks in exchange for a high-power, high-prestige career?

Stress is the negative buzzword of modern life. "I'm so stressed out over this project that I can't sleep," one patient tells me. "Between cooking, cleaning, organizing the kids, and working part time," says another, "the stress is killing me." Yet another complains, "I'm putting so much effort into stress reduction that it's added a whole new level of tension!" For all the griping, however, there's an undercurrent of smugness in each of these statements, as if the mere fact of experiencing stress is a mark of valor. If I'm stressed out, they seem to be saying, I must deserve to succeed.

The misunderstanding is twofold. There's the assumption that all stress is unpleasant and the assumption that one has to be overstressed — or distressed — to succeed.

In fact, all stress is not unpleasant, and only some forms of stress are necessary to success. In the strictest sense, stress is nothing more than emotional and physical arousal. We experience stress when we are excited, enthusiastic, or sexually enticed, and when faced with emergency situations or tough problems. Without stress, we would be ill-equipped to manage in a crisis or under pressure or to experience our full range of emotions.

What distinguishes positive from negative stress, or distress, is the level of arousal. If you become so upset that you get a migraine headache and cannot function, your stress level is too high to be healthy. If you are so panicked by a situation that you become numb or severely depressed, your stress level is too low to be healthy. When you operate at an excessively high or low stress level for a lengthy period of time, you can develop chronic stress-related illnesses, such as ulcers, back pain, high blood pressure, or heart disease. Emotionally, you'll feel burned out. Personally, you're likely to withdraw from or alienate the people closest to you. And professionally, you're likely to experience a decline in performance that corresponds directly to your level of distress.

The real key to stress management is to find the zone of stress that enhances your performance and your outlook on life, that contributes to your physical and emotional fitness instead of undermining it. Once you've identified this zone, regular exercise and relaxation, improved nutrition, time management, and stress-reduction techniques can help you protect it. Numerous books describe these techniques in detail, and I encourage you to consult them. My purpose here is simply to alert you to the importance of a balanced approach that recognizes both the value and the dangers of stress.

7. Sheer willpower versus the ability to recognize and capitalize on good luck

Do you feel that good things happen only to other people, never to you?

Do you believe you can achieve anything you desire, if you just want it badly enough?

Do you automatically blame yourself when you are unable to reach a particular goal?

True success is not determined entirely by luck, nor is it purely a matter of willpower. Good fortune does play a role, but what really counts is your ability to recognize and seize whatever golden opportunities come your way.

Many of my patients resist this notion. They prefer to cast themselves either as pawns of fate, abdicating responsibility, or as masters of their own destinies, giving themselves too much responsibility. Both views are out of balance and tend to work against internal success by inducing a sense of resignation on the one hand, and of liability on the other. When the fatalist achieves, he can take little pride or satisfaction in his success. When the self-willed person fails, he may become so mired in irrational guilt and self-condemnation that he cannot see the real problems before him.

We all know people who seem to have incredibly good luck, and others whose lives seem clouded in misfortune. We also know that some who are born with enormous advantages squander them, while others who start with almost insurmountable hardships become heroes for us all. The distinction between success and failure lies less in luck than in your ability to utilize positive opportunities and shift direction when obstacles are genuinely beyond your control.

8. Absolute consistency versus flexibility

Does the prospect of change make you uncomfortable?
Do you defend your decisions even when you know you're wrong?
How do you see yourself twenty years from now?

Do you think that successful people are always right, always in control, and always know exactly where they're going? These are dangerous illusions, because they imply that success demands a degree of certainty that no one can sustain.

The notion of success as an absolute tends to frighten off those who recognize their own insecurity or confusion. "If I can't envision myself as a corporate president or CEO," one patient told me, "I have no business becoming a manager." When I asked her why not, she replied, "I'll never get ahead if I question myself and my motives. If I'm going to succeed in any profession, I've got to be completely sure of my target and I have to have a clear, fail-safe strategy for achieving it. Unless I have it all together, I won't be able to stand up against the competition." Though she didn't realize it, this patient was using a common avoidance tactic that promised to keep her from ever realizing her dreams. By setting impossible standards, particularly the standards of absolute self-knowledge and consistency, she was keeping herself in a comfortable holding pattern, waiting as if for spiritual enlightenment to reveal her own perfect truth.

The illusion of absolute consistency is also responsible for many mid-career casualties. The artist who has pursued a single, cohesive theme for many years becomes attracted to different artistic forms and issues, but cannot bring himself to pursue them because the change would threaten his professional identity, perhaps resulting in a drop in sales and puzzling his friends and critics. The executive who is known for her methodical research and analytic thinking suddenly has an inspired marketing idea that cannot be substantiated by data, and though her intuition tells her she is right, she is unwilling to trust her feeling. When consistency takes priority over inspiration and necessity, it can lead to stagnation.

In fact, it's wise to question yourself all the time, challenging what you think you know and asking what you need to learn. When faced with tough decisions, accept that there may be several right answers — or none — and base your choices on issues and evidence as well as your personal convictions. This approach requires a certain amount of flexibility because while your beliefs may never waver, the circumstances surrounding each decision are constantly shifting. There is no perfect recipe for success; the moment you think there is, you'll find that the ingredients have changed.

9. Systematic versus creative thinking

Do you think there are some things you just can't learn to do well?

Do you allow yourself to act on impulse, or do you resist impulsive behavior?

Do you look for solutions from outside your immediate area of expertise?

In his autobiography Lee Iacocca blames the decline of the Ford Motor Company during the 1970s on the "bean counters" — business school managers with "financial minds and impressive analytical skills" who "tend to be defensive, conservative, and pessimistic" and "are always cautioning you on why you shouldn't" take an aggressive or speculative position.[6] With their systematic thinking and rejection of risk, such financial analysts promise stability and security, but as Iacocca points out, stability and security do not always add up to progress or growth, particularly in the face of rapidly changing conditions and demands.

Iacocca was addressing the effects of the bean-counting mentality on business, but the hazards of overly systematic thinking extend to the individual as well. Just as managerial dependence on strict logic and measurable proof can stifle the growth of a corporation, systematic thinking, when it preempts creative thinking, can impede personal growth. After all, the richness of life depends on the richness of our minds. Without a constant flow of fresh ideas and options, we come to a deadening halt.

Creative — or Renaissance — thinking uses all the senses, both the left and right sides of the brain, and resources within and outside the body. It extends back in time and forward into the future. It pulls inspiration from all vocational fields and academic disciplines. By accepting input from every possible source, the Renaissance thinker learns to mix and match information, to make connections and develop ideas that would never occur to the purely systematic thinker. The Renaissance thinker has a broader vision and therefore approaches problems with greater insight and a wider range of solutions. Eventually, of course, there must be some systematic basis for selecting the best option, but this refining process is productive only if the preliminary brainstorming has produced an array of creative ideas.

The systematic thinker, basing decisions on facts and figures, tends to say "I can't," while the Renaissance thinker, always searching for new possibilities, tends to say "Why not?" Many of my patients claim that they cannot do what they really want to do because they are "not qualified." One woman desperately loved ballet but insisted she'd never be able to make a career in dance because she hadn't begun studying ballet until college, she didn't have the right connections, she'd never be able to support herself by dancing, and so on. She was so busy systematically ticking off all the negatives that she completely lost sight of the other, encouraging factors: her passion for dance as an art form, her intuitive grasp of choreography, and her natural gift for critiquing other dancers. Once she began taking a creative approach to the problem, brainstorming all possible options and ramifications, the barriers began to shrink and she was able to plan several different courses of action, all related to her love of dance. Finally, after determining that she was attracted primarily by the world of dance as opposed to the act of performing, she faced three appealing alternatives: teaching, choreographing, or writing. For a couple of years she did all three, teaching a class for teenagers, composing her own dances for a fledgling company, and providing dance notes for the local paper. These activities cross-fed each other, helping her build a reputation as a dance expert that eventually landed her one job as dance critic for a national dance magazine and another teaching choreography at a large liberal arts college.

It's important to note that creativity is not actively rewarded in all professions or by all employers. As Iacocca's example of

Ford in the seventies demonstrates, many firms prefer bean counters. If your sole goal is to be an executive in such a firm, Renaissance thinking may do little to advance your cause. However, if you intend to survive in a position of real leadership, you have to know how to find creative as well as sensible solutions. But the real value of Renaissance thinking lies in its effect on your whole life, not just your professional career. By taking chances and defying linear logic, you may discover new inspiration in the most unexpected sources.

10. Pragmatism versus idealism

> Do you feel powerless to change your life?
> Are you more concerned about the present or the future?
> Do you ask what you can do for society, or what society can do for you?

Pragmatists focus on the world as it is, idealists on the world as it should be. Which approach enjoys the greater success? This question has been batted around throughout civilization. Up until the Renaissance, the idealists clearly led public opinion. For the Greeks, success served the ideal of citizenship. The Romans idealized excellence in service of the Republic. The early Christians idealized service to God. But with the increasing secularization of life since the fifteenth century, external success has become an ambition without a cause — and with increasingly hollow spiritual rewards.

The pragmatist myth of success presumes spiritual complacency and material greed. The end objective is not to make the world a better place or even to achieve a high level of personal awareness, but to take the best that the existing world has to offer for personal consumption. This attitude has never been more pervasive than it is today. It lurks beneath the frenzy of leveraged buyouts in the business world. It provides the rationalization for industry to pollute and devour our natural resources and for nations to stockpile nuclear weaponry. And it pressures class after class of college students to place financial profit ahead of social conscience in selecting a professional field.

It is also responsible for the rising rates of depression and disillusionment among those who, by all accounts, are "most likely to succeed." There is a sense of confinement in this view of success, and the more pragmatic you are, the more acutely you feel the squeeze.

If you lack a sense of vision and moral involvement, the pursuits of material wealth, fame, and power are purely superficial exercises.

While pragmatism sentences us to conditions as they are, idealism inspires us to invest in change. It gives us a personal stake in the future as well as the present. It gives us a sense of continuity and purpose, a sense that we are making a difference and that there is a point to our being alive. It makes us feel that we are active participants instead of victims of circumstance. And it reassures us that true success has no boundaries.

LEARNING TO THRIVE: THE INTEGRATED LIFE

We can only have the highest happiness, such as goes along with true greatness, by having wide thoughts and much feeling for the rest of the world as well as ourselves.

— *George Eliot*

IT IS ONE THING to understand the components of true success; it is quite another to lead a truly successful life. Living success involves action, conviction, and self-knowledge, commodities that you alone can supply. There is no single path to fulfillment, for each of us has different passions and needs. Ultimately, however, our sense of success boils down to one vital principle: personal integrity.

By integrity I do not just mean being morally upright and honest, although that certainly is important. Integrity also means being unified and cohesive. A house has integrity when all the environmental and construction elements support each other physically, functionally, and stylistically. A company has integrity when labor and management share the same commitment to quality and abide by the principles of conduct of the surrounding community. We as individuals have integrity when our values, ambitions, and actions work together, giving us a sense of inner harmony as well as harmony with the world in which we live. In short, having integrity means leading an integrated life in dealing with ourselves and with others.

One of the signals that you're approaching the edge of success is the feeling that your life is in pieces and that you, as a person, are moving in umpteen different directions. Unfortunately, given the hectic pace and competitiveness of modern life, this is an all-too-common situation. But slowing down and withdrawing from the rat race are neither realistic nor, necessarily, effective solutions. Despite the popularity of Bobby McFerrin's 1988 hit single, "Don't Worry, Be Happy," this advice is far too simplistic to be useful. Most of us can't afford to simply shrug away our cares, and even if we could, ignoring them isn't going to bring us any closer to true happiness. The challenge runs deeper than that. We achieve fulfillment by facing those worries and resolving them through active engagement, not by denying them through complacency.

If you feel that your life is more fragmented than integrated, you may need to reconceptualize your choices and your actions. The following guidelines can help you begin this process.

Balancing Your Life View

Do you need to change professions? Should you get a divorce? Is it time to start a family? Do you spend too much time exercising — or not enough? Would you be happier if you changed your lifestyle? These are just a few of the questions that may loom near the edge of success. They reflect core feelings of uncertainty and dissatisfaction that demand some kind of change.

But does the change have to involve a major overhaul of your professional career, family, or personal life? Not always. You may well have all the right components for a satisfying life and simply need to bring them into balance. So before you quit your job and move to a log cabin, give yourself a grace period in which to explore more moderate solutions. Try to incorporate one of the following ten suggestions into your life each day. If circumstances make it impossible for you to adopt these principles, you may need to use the more specific strategy for change outlined at the end of this chapter. For most people, however, personal success is not that difficult to achieve; it simply requires some fine-tuning of attitude and organization.

THE TEN PRINCIPLES OF TRUE SUCCESS

1. Be honest about yourself.
2. Take responsibility for yourself.
3. Separate your needs from your desires.
4. Consider life as a network of connected but undivided units.
5. Build on the past.
6. Make every moment count.
7. Maintain a balance of routine and spontaneity.
8. Consider yourself a unique but connected member of the human community.
9. Chart your own success course.
10. Accept failure as an opportunity for change.

1. Be honest about yourself.

One of the most popular myths in America holds that we can all be and have whatever our hearts desire. If you just want it badly enough, you too can become a millionaire, run a corporation, fly to the moon, or become President. There is a conspiracy of sorts, dominated by the media, politicians, and "new age" therapists, that encourages us to buy into this illusion because it supports their sales pitches — You can be anything you want to be *if* . . . you wear the right cologne, vote for the right candidate, or follow the right guru. But as tempting as it is to believe that we can command our own destinies, each of us possesses a unique blend of strengths and weaknesses, opportunities and limitations, many of which cannot be altered by using the right product or changing philosophies. Denying this basic fact to sustain the fantasy of unlimited possibility is like walking on thin ice. There's a chance you will make it all the way across, but you have no way of knowing or controlling whether you'll arrive safely.

If you are honest about yourself, you cannot accept the myth of unlimited possibility. Given your particular physical, intellectual, and emotional makeup, there are certain paths open to you, and there are some that inevitably are going to disappoint you. The more accurate your self-perception, the more appropriate your chosen course is likely to be. The more appropriate your course, the more successful you are likely to be.

This is not to say that you should resign yourself to poverty forever just because you were born in a tenement, or that you're doomed to domestic servitude because you happen to be female. Environmental and cultural circumstances are just one part of the total picture. The internal forces that motivate you and define your personal values and beliefs are much more potent factors. Given the initiative, creativity, skill, and faith, you can override incredibly difficult obstacles, even including an abused or deprived childhood. However, if you enjoy working alone and feel uncomfortable in large groups, it makes little sense to fantasize about being in charge of a huge corporation. If you thrive on the action and excitement of a high-powered professional career and the rest of your life is prospering as well, you are probably not going to be happy for long in a contemplative, pastoral setting. If you get caught up in a position or fantasy that's inconsistent with your true nature, you are bound to feel the conflict, even if you succeed externally.

Your chances of external success drop, however, when you're not being straight with yourself. When you're uncomfortable or distracted, your judgment inevitably flags. You may have trouble telling positive risks from negative ones. You may lack the decisiveness to resolve problems. Even when you are technically qualified for a given role, if you do not *feel* qualified and committed, you are not going to function at your best.

To keep yourself in line, it's a good idea to make a complete personal appraisal every year or so. Include your physical, intellectual, and emotional characteristics — strengths and weaknesses. Then construct a similar profile of the characteristics you must have to meet your personal goals and another of the traits your professional goals demand. If the three lists are similar, there's consistency between your real self and your desired self, which means that your goals are reasonable. If all three lists are different, or your personal traits fulfill only one of your other profiles, then something may need to change to bring your three faces closer together. However, before you begin remodeling your life, go back and examine your three profiles objectively, consulting a friend or family member, if necessary, to make sure your responses are accurate. Most of us have a tendency to identify ourselves so closely with one realm — usually work — that we have trouble honestly appraising our performance in different areas. We may also under- or overestimate what's demanded of us in certain roles. These three profiles can serve as references as you proceed through the rest of this chapter, but they are only as useful as they are honest.

2. *Take responsibility for yourself.*

Success is often viewed as unlimited leisure and freedom. "When I'm successful, no one will tell me what to do," one aggressively ambitious patient told me. "I'll be totally free." He was wrong on both counts. Had he but realized it, he was already free and responsible for himself. He had chosen to pursue a high-powered career that ran him ragged, yet he could just as easily choose a less pressured existence. A bachelor, he did not have the added consideration of a wife or children. The only thing restraining him was his own conventionality; he had boxed himself into a concept of success focused solely on career prestige.

Success is not a condition of freedom, and it does not buy irresponsibility. To this young man, "No one will tell me what to do" meant being in absolute control, owing nothing to anyone, taking orders from no one. In essence, it meant total isolation, because even the most powerful leaders ultimately take orders from the people and conditions surrounding them. If they ignore the needs and sentiments of others, they are quickly toppled from power. If they deny their responsibility to family, friends, and community, they are eventually rejected. The resulting feelings of alienation and loneliness quickly shatter the illusion of success.

Taking responsibility for yourself means utilizing the freedom you already possess to grow and develop. It means acting on the basis of judgment, not habit or assumption. And it encompasses not just what you do for yourself but also what you do for those around you. As your capacity for responsibility grows, so does your sense of importance and meaning. This is the real substance of success.

3. Separate your needs from your desires.

We commonly mix up desires and needs so that we lose sight of what's truly essential. Because this confusion tends to distort our definition of success, it's important to step back every now and then and separate the things we genuinely need from those

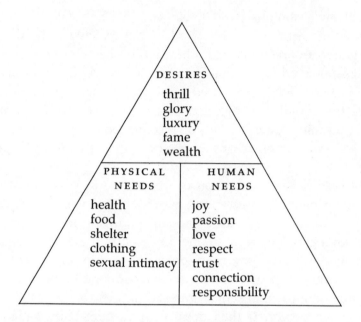

we don't need but simply desire. In a general way, the hierarchy can be depicted as a pyramid.

Plutarch wrote, "That state of life is most happy where super-fluities are not required, and necessaries are not wanting." To feel truly successful, we all must satisfy the needs on the first level of the pyramid. Then if we go on to achieve those ultimate desires — or superfluities — fine, but they are not the real basis of happiness. If we chase after our desires without first fulfilling our physical and human needs, we are likely to succeed only in making ourselves miserable.

Many people set goals that reflect their desires but contradict their needs. One of my patients was constantly setting targets that forced him to strain past his limits. "I have to set goals for myself," he declared, "or I won't have any sense of accomplishment." One day he would push himself to run two miles, the next, three. Within two weeks he was up to seven miles. Within four he had torn a ligament and couldn't run for three months. The pattern repeated itself in his other hobbies and on the job. A car salesman, he habitually set impossible goals for himself. Predictably, he usually fell short, which caused him to be depressed and irritable with his family and friends. Those habitual goals were doing him in because they were set by his desires rather than his needs.

Once the compulsive athlete stopped measuring his performance by distance and speed, and instead worked at sustaining his target heart rate for a reasonable period of time, he found that he enjoyed his workouts more, sustained fewer injuries, and was more enthusiastic about sticking with his exercise program. When he applied the same principles at work and began setting sales goals that reflected what he needed to earn to satisfy his personal needs and to advance in the dealership, he discovered that moderate performance targets allowed him to succeed far more often, which in turn kept him on a much more positive emotional keel at home and netted him a higher income at the end of the year. In the end, he achieved most of his desires, not by pursuing them exclusively but by making sure his basic needs were met first, then moving ahead incrementally.

4. *Consider life as a network of connected but undivided units.*
Aristotle wrote that "we should be able, not only to work well, but to use leisure well."[1] In his design, play and rest are necessary for us to work well, and work in turn is necessary to support leisure. For Aristotle, leisure encompassed family and community involvement, but this definition clouds the importance of these human relationships. A more accurate picture of true success would separate family and community into separate priorities, with self and family as the core and community as the context, as shown in the following illustration.

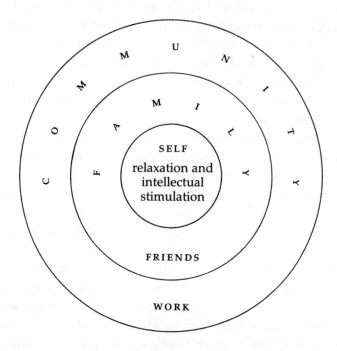

Protecting your commitment to one unit may mean regulating your commitment to another. You have to learn to say no. Faced with an escalating conflict between work obligations and his family, business consultant Tom Peters developed a set of rules to safeguard his personal priorities. First, he schedules no work commitments on weekends, and out-of-town engagements only on Tuesdays through Thursdays. Second, he cuts out all unnecessary meetings and social engagements. Third, he's adopted a pay-but-don't-go policy to deal with the invitations to charity dinners and cultural events that seem to multiply with professional achievement.[2] By restructuring his schedule to minimize waste, Peters came up with a plan that could serve as a model for many of us.

Another consideration is the effect of technology on our lives. So-called efficiency devices such as portable office equipment, cellular phones, and personal beepers can be tools of convenience or instruments of self-abuse. It's no coincidence that 1989 polls show Americans working six hours more per week than they did before the recent boom in portable office equipment or that we have some ten hours less of leisure time each week than we did fifteen years ago. But we are not obligated to turn our homes into offices or surrender our vacation time just because the technology is available to work around the clock. When torn between reading your child a bedtime story and attending to the unedited report that's beckoning from your laptop computer, ask yourself which is *really* more important. If your laptop holds more power over you than your family, something is radically out of whack.

5. Build on the past.

It's easy to belittle the events and accomplishments of your past. As an accountant in your thirties you may feel a little embarrassed about your attempt to become a stand-up comedian right out of college. Having graduated with a degree in engineering, you may have completely forgotten your childhood dream of becoming a great novelist. We have a tendency to get so caught up in our immediate lives that we dismiss the forces and impulses that shaped us. In the process, we lose a valuable resource for the future.

The past holds much vital information. It can tell you why you react to conflict in a particular way. It can help you understand your fears and desires. It can reassure you in moments of self-doubt. It contains interests, abilities, and ideas that may guide you in periods of transition. You may even find the inspiration for a new career or hobby by reexamining the passions of your youth. But perhaps most important of all, the past provides a sense of continuity that can comfort you and give you strength.

It might help to think of your past in terms of files. Each file contains a passage of your life, a personal observation, even sensory bits, like the aroma of burning leaves you associate with a particular day in some childhood autumn. You don't keep all the files open all the time. That would create such clutter you wouldn't be able to function. But you don't want to throw away this vital information either, for that would effectively erase part of yourself. The best solution is to learn to manage your personal files just as you would vital office data. Organize them in your mind, put the least relevant ones in deep storage, and review those which relate directly to your present life. Pull out the insights, feelings, and ideas that may be useful, and return the rest to a drawer within easy reach. Even episodes that you want to forget, like being the victim of abuse or crime, may someday prove useful if you know how to access them. By managing the past, you eliminate the need to hide from it.

The past is not entirely contained in memories, of course. Much of it lives on in traditions and cherished objects, the stories you tell about your childhood, the rituals and ideas you pass on to your own children. By keeping these memories active, you weave a sense of unity and endurance that can strengthen your whole family for generations to come.

6. Make every moment count.

Are you driven because you're being pressured by forces beyond your control — by economic or social forces from outside, perhaps, or by confusion and fear from within? Or have you made a conscious choice to create real value through your actions? The contrast is between busyness and productive activity.

According to the German philosopher Hegel, "Life has a value only when it has something valuable as its object." The sense of value is tangible when you are engaged in productive activity. You make a personal investment in the process of your actions, and you feel connected to the outcome of your efforts. This engagement produces a strong sense of continuity over time and increases the frequency and intensity of discovery. To take a simple example, which also illustrates how this process can affect our perceptions of daily life, consider the way you look at a flower. Do you simply read it as a spot of color and shape, or do you really *see* it — how it fits into the surrounding garden, how its color subtly shifts in the play of light and shadow, how the moisture collects on its petals, how the pollen lies tentatively on stamen and pistil? If you look with busy eyes, the flower is merely an object. If your eyes and mind are active, the flower is a miracle.

The value that we perceive most keenly comes not from creating or originating a particular commodity but from the internal activity of observation, inquiry, and discovery. You don't have to take physical possession of a beautiful flower to absorb its value. You don't have to produce a masterpiece to savor the act of painting. And you don't have to own a company to appreciate the complex weave of talent, information, inspiration, and cooperation that makes the enterprise move forward.

You also increase the value of your life by facing events, people, and problems in a direct, positive manner. The actor James Coco had an interesting technique for reducing the level of anger in his life. Each month he would list twenty-five things that made him furious, including ancient vendettas, simmering grievances, and incidental altercations. Then he would confront one item from the list each day and ask himself why it made him so angry. If he couldn't come up with a rationally defensible reason, he would cross it off the list. In this way he eliminated minor incidents, feuds that had occurred too long ago to matter, and conflicts based on jealousy, envy, or unrealistic expectations. At the end of each month he had a much abbreviated list that contained only the problems that truly justified his anger. Then, because he was no longer wasting energy on irrelevant rage, he could channel his anger into constructive efforts to resolve those specific issues.

Consider how you feel when you work through a tough problem at work or resolve a personal dispute with a friend. Now consider how you feel when you try to deny or run away from pain and confusion. Perhaps your boss has given you an assignment you think you can't handle, so you put it at the bottom of your "to do" pile and make excuses whenever he asks if you've completed it. Or maybe your teenage son has just insulted you, and though you feel like decking him, you give him the silent treatment and then lapse into despair. Running away or running circles around pain and conflict only prolongs your suffering and makes it more difficult to heal the wound. Confronting your troubles directly and immediately, on the other hand, increases the chance of resolution and gives you the satisfaction of acting on your feelings. If you have difficulty with this idea, imagine that your boss or son is about to die and today is to be your final time together. Do you want to spend it in subterfuge and stifled rage, or do you want to settle your problems and move on?

7. Maintain a balance of routine and spontaneity.

Many of my patients who appear outwardly successful complain either that they never do anything new and exciting or that they are moving so fast they've forgotten what they really want out of life. Both groups feel frustrated and dissatisfied with their accomplishments. Both assume they must completely reverse their lifestyles to achieve satisfaction. But what each of these groups *really* needs is to moderate its routines.

A certain amount of regularity in life makes us feel secure and in control. It helps to keep us organized and focused and provides stability, which can have a surprisingly healing effect on emotional pain, grief, and jealousy. Two Yale psychologists found that the fastest way to mend a broken heart is simply to go through the motions of daily life and concentrate on your routine. Yielding to the impulse to withdraw and analyze what went wrong apparently does little to soothe the pain or return you to normal.[3]

Too much regularity, of course, can be numbing. We all need to break out on occasion, to stretch in new directions and act a little wild. Spontaneity is an essential component of creativity and discovery. Yet we have to be selective with our impulses, or we're liable to end up buried in debt and out of a job.

The trick is to use our routines as a framework for spontaneity, much as a scientist specifies the time, place, and governing conditions in which to conduct "spontaneous" experiments. It's not really a matter of saying, "I'll set aside Saturdays to do whatever I want," but of making an allowance for curiosity and playfulness in everyday life. As with the scientist, this may require extra planning to accommodate impulsiveness. For instance, if you're in the library doing research on a project that's due in an hour, you cannot afford to get sidetracked by unrelated books that catch your eye. If you begin your research several days in advance, however, you can take several breaks to peruse the shelves and still not compromise your research. As simplistic as this example may sound, it demonstrates how we sometimes unconsciously box ourselves in, and how easy it can be to break those boxes open.

8. Consider yourself a unique but connected member of the human community.

Many people misinterpret the popular psychological concept of self-actualization as a defense of selfishness. I often hear patients insisting that their only responsibility is to "be true to themselves." One, a shoplifter, felt that she was being true to herself by ripping off the Establishment, but she was also hurting the other shoppers, who would ultimately have to pay higher prices to compensate for her theft. Likewise, a middle-aged father asserted that he was being true to himself by walking out on his wife and four kids to follow his guru to India, but the price of his personal "enlightenment" was the devastation of his family. Seemingly at the other end of the spectrum, an ambitious middle manager believed he was simply claiming his due by undermining his coworkers to get the next promotion, but his penalty was alienation, mistrust, and the resentment of his colleagues.

We don't operate in a vacuum. Virtually everything we do, from running a company to flushing a toilet, has an impact elsewhere in the human community, and everything that occurs within the community has an effect on us. We cannot be truly successful if we live in total isolation or turn our backs on the people who love us. We cannot genuinely thrive if we have dropped out — socially, morally, or emotionally — of the world around us. In this regard, the standard of true success is not harmfulness or even harmlessness, but helpfulness.

Helping, in this sense, does not have to involve charity, but it does involve a sense of social responsibility. An example of non-charitable social conscience can be found in the new trend of ethical or social investing, known as SI. Particularly popular among women, environmentalists, and investors concerned about human rights and demilitarization, SI takes four forms.

Avoidance investors refuse to put money into firms that violate certain basic principles, such as companies that do business with South Africa. *Affirmative investors* buy stocks and bonds of companies with laudable conduct records. *Community investments* are deposits in local financial institutions that lend to worthy community projects, such as early childhood education or environmental cleanup campaigns. *Shareholder activism* involves buying shares in a firm with an objectionable record and then, as an active shareholder, pressuring the company to change its policies. Socially conscious investments do not produce lower earnings than other investments. Over the past decade, they have averaged returns of up to four times those of the Dow Jones industrial average.[4]

Too often we forget how much our personal happiness depends on the community's wellness. It takes a personal or national disaster to remind us how frail we are as individuals without the protection of a healthy, stable society. Sensitivity to the community usually increases directly with personal need: the laborer who is making a fair wage and is ahead with his mortgage payments resents having to pay into Social Security and says the poor are just lazy, but when his plant closes and he can't find employment, his fierce individualism is silenced by his need for community support. Similarly, war often mobilizes even the most self-centered people to make heroic sacrifices. The tragedy is that the very disasters that bring out the best in us are often created by the worst in us. The only way to break the cycle is to build an ongoing spirit of community and global involvement that inhibits selfishness and promotes shared responsibility and respect for the world we all inhabit.

9. Chart your own success course.

This entire book is about redefining success in your own terms. But it's difficult to challenge patterns that everyone else accepts without question. Even having read this far, you still may equate promotions with success. You still may have trouble believing that your plumber could be as fulfilled as the President of the United States or that the chairman of your company could feel less successful than you.

The best way to crack these barriers is to chart your own success course. Ask yourself what particular milestones you must reach to fulfill your ambitions, abilities, and values. These may or may not follow a typical career track, so watch out for those "automatic" milestones. Most great scholars, inventors, and artists attain great stature, but they would not make great presidents or board chairmen. Becoming prominent in your field does not have to mean going on the lecture circuit, unless you consider lecturing a meaningful activity. Being the most important person in your company does not automatically mean that you manage the company's business affairs. Your success depends on your ability to see how your particular achievements build on one another and to keep the structure intact, even if it means defying standard operating procedures or turning down a promotion.

It's also important to recognize the true value of the rewards you do amass as your career develops. Olympic diving champion Greg Louganis once explained that he had taken his reputation for granted until one day when he saw a young boy smoking in the parking lot after watching him practice. "What are you doing?" Louganis asked the boy. "I want to be just like you," answered the child. In that moment the Olympian understood both the responsibility and the opportunity his success had earned him. He immediately stopped smoking and began to present himself as a positive role model for his young admirers.

Money, too, can be valuable or destructive, depending on how you incorporate it into your life. The true value of money lies not in its face amount but in the possibilities it can open up. To use money as a real success tool you have to be willing and able to spend it constructively, not simply for your own pleasure or aggrandizement but in ways that support your ideals and your dreams.

10. Accept failure as an opportunity for change.
We are conditioned to resist and resent failure of any kind. But there are several different types of failure, not all of which are necessarily bad. Before you can effectively manage success, then, you need to understand the varieties of failure.

Noble failure involves a valiant attempt in the name of a cause. Mohandas Gandhi was not always successful in his efforts to stop the bloodshed between India's warring factions in the months before that nation's independence, but he was revered for his attempts. Noble failures generate self-respect, earn the admiration of others, and strengthen your integrity.

Necessary failure occurs when the price of achievement is too high. Accepting this kind of failure involves judgment and choice, as generals, politicians, and business leaders know all too well. In the interest of sanity and decency, it is better to lose a battle than to lose the lives of everyone in the battalion. In the interest of democracy, it is better to accept defeat in a fair election than to mount a coup against the winner. In the name of efficiency and economy, it is better to discontinue a product than to hurl it at an indifferent market.

Failure is ultimately damaging only if it involves deceit, ineptitude, or greed. When the desire to prevail is allowed to override decency and common sense, it constitutes a personal failure, whether you win or lose. The same is true when you are so unwilling to appear a failure that you refuse to accept responsibility for your actions.

The most common mistakes we make can be classified as *instructive failures*. Based on honest but erroneous assumptions or mistaken perceptions, these failures let us know that we have to change our thinking or behavior. They challenge us to search through the rubble to find what went wrong and develop a plan to prevent the same thing from happening again. In some cases the best response is to make some adjustments and press on toward the original goal. In others it makes sense to break the task into small, manageable chunks and attack them one at a time instead of all together. And in still others, the most sensible decision is to strike out in an entirely new direction. You face the same options whether the setback occurs in your job, marriage, friendships, or exercise regimen. The important thing is to view the situation as an opportunity rather than a threat. Failure is no excuse for surrender.

A Strategy for Initiation and Change

If you are having difficulty applying the principles of success to your life, you may need to make some changes, but don't try to make a radical shift overnight. To be effective, change usually has to be a gradual process, so take the time to plan your course of action thoroughly before attempting to implement it.

The following strategy shows the kind of thinking that must go into any major life change, whether it involves your individual habits, your family or social relationships, or your work. The case of Peter, an overworked insurance executive who felt he was neglecting his five-year-old son, illustrates how these guidelines can be translated into action.

1. Identify the problem in objective terms.

Peter started by complaining of several related problems. His son, Jimmy, was growing up too fast. He resented his company for working him so hard. He didn't feel he was a good father. Peter needed to sort through all these subjective reactions to get to the objective issue, which was that he was not spending enough time with Jimmy.

2. Identify the goal.

Having defined the basic problem, Peter found that his goal was quite simple: find a way to spend more time with Jimmy. We decided that was still too vague, so after weighing several different ideals, we settled on a more specific target: Peter wanted to spend as much time with Jimmy as necessary to establish a close, trusting father-son relationship.

3. Identify the problem in subjective terms.

It was easy for Peter to blame his dilemma on his job, but if he was going to find an effective solution, he had to understand the internal conflicts that were contributing to the problem. Jimmy was five years old, after all, and Peter had waited until then to admit his frustration. Why? Because part of him was reluctant to be a more involved father. When Jimmy was a baby, Peter hadn't wanted to change his son's diapers or deal with the nighttime crying. Though he considered himself egalitarian, he still took it for granted that his wife was in charge of the distasteful chores of child care. As Jimmy got older, Peter had balked at the idea of watching *Sesame Street* or cartoons for hours on end, and he was unnerved by the disciplinary issues that emerged. And there was always the fear that if he got more involved he'd somehow mess Jimmy up — or get so enthralled with the child that he'd push his wife out of the picture. These fears were not necessarily rational or obvious, but they were definite factors in Peter's choice to absent himself from his son's first few years. Now he had to confront them at the same time he was confronting his deeper fear that Jimmy would grow up hating, misunderstanding, or simply not knowing him. Peter was haunted by Harry Chapin's song "The Cat's in the Cradle." He did not want to lose his son's love through neglect.

4. Generate possible solutions.

Here was Peter's chance to use his creativity. He came up with a host of options, including several — like taking his wife and Jimmy on a year-long trip around the world — that were unrealistic but fun to think about. Among his more plausible suggestions:

▾ He could get up early and make breakfast for Jimmy every morning.
▾ He could take Jimmy fishing for a month every summer.
▾ He could spend all day every Saturday with Jimmy.
▾ He could set aside an hour each night to watch TV with Jimmy.
▾ He could take Jimmy to work with him during school vacations.

5. Look at the pros and cons of each option.

Peter was ready to institute all his solutions immediately until he backed up and examined them more carefully. It was fine to plan to get up at six each morning, but he was normally a late sleeper, and he was very grumpy in the morning even when he got enough sleep. Would he and Jimmy really have any meaningful conversations if he was in his usual morning temper? Also, the only thing he had for breakfast was coffee, and he didn't like to prepare even that. His wife would probably appreciate his efforts, but she was an early riser and didn't really need his help in the morning.

After subjecting each alternative to the same kind of scrutiny, Peter realized that Jimmy didn't like fishing enough to make it a summer tradition; if he watched TV every night, he'd want to watch the ball games, and Jimmy wasn't interested in doing that; taking Jimmy to the office would be fun the first couple of times, but at age five Jimmy was unlikely to be interested in the insurance business, and Peter wouldn't have much time to spend with him at work. And in order to spend Saturday with Jimmy, Peter would have to reschedule his Saturday basketball game and do more work at night to clear the time.

6. Choose a solution.

While all of Peter's ideas were good in theory, the only one that would work as a *regular* practice was to spend Saturdays with his son. On the weekend, Peter could turn himself off from work and really concentrate on Jimmy, doing different things each week or, if Jimmy wanted, signing up for a regular class or activity. Sometimes they could spend time as a family, but with Peter on duty, his wife could also take the day off if she wanted. The plan would work for everyone.

7. Decide how to implement the plan.

First Peter would have to discuss the idea with his wife and Jimmy. Then he'd have to find another time for his basketball game or substitute a run early Saturday mornings. He could either stay later at the office or do more work at home during week-nights to get caught up before the weekend. Finally, he and Jimmy would have to plan their activities together. Initially Peter had trouble with the last step. He was sold on the idea of spending time together, but how was he going to *fill* that time? Peter had to come up with a list of his own before he approached Jimmy. Once he had a group of options that appealed to him — seeing a mutually interesting movie, playing ball in the park, having lunch out, swimming at the Y — Peter regained his confidence and enthusiasm.

8. Weed out unrealistic expectations.

In Peter's mind he and Jimmy would have a ball every Satur-day. Jimmy would be on his best behavior and tell Peter what a great dad he was. Peter, in turn, would shower Jimmy with un-conditional affection and be a perfect role model for the boy. But would he want out of the deal if Jimmy had one of his rare tan-trums during their time together? What if they couldn't agree on an activity? What if Peter was preoccupied with a problem at work and just couldn't concentrate on Jimmy? Considering these real possibilities and the disappointment he would feel if they occurred, Peter understood that he had to moderate his expec-tations. To make the plan work he would have to be prepared for both good times and bad. It had to be enough to spend the time together and get to know each other better. By creating a broader, less demanding view of success, Peter reduced the chances that he would give up prematurely.

9. Plan for self-sabotage.

Peter wanted to believe that he'd leap out of bed every Satur-day and whisk Jimmy off for one adventure after another. But he didn't have to reach far below the surface to figure out how he might sabotage the plan. He might bring home a pile of work that had to be finished before Sunday. He might stay up late on Friday and be too tired to take Jimmy the next morning. He might get so caught up in problems at the office that he couldn't concentrate on Jimmy when Saturday rolled around. He might accept invitations to go out with his wife or buddies on Saturday. Once he thought through these maneuvers, he realized how easy it would be to back out on Jimmy without being aware of what he was doing. By facing himself down this way, he added a layer of resolve that just might prevent him from using any of these maneuvers.

10. Develop alternative plans.

For all the preparation, there remained the chance that his Saturday plan might not work out. What then? Peter had to come up with a plan that would compensate on a temporary basis — if he was out of town one weekend, for example. He also needed alternatives in the event his first plan didn't work — if, say, Jimmy preferred to spend every Saturday with his friends. Looking back to his original list of options, Peter decided that on occasional weeks when Saturday didn't work out, he would get up early and make breakfast for Jimmy. If Jimmy vetoed the Saturday plan or if something else came up regularly, Peter would come home early at least two nights a week and spend that extra time with his son. If necessary he would stay up later those nights and do his work after Jimmy was in bed.

The final step, of course, was to put the plan into action and face the consequences. Peter found that Jimmy was not always attentive or cooperative simply because his father had taken the time to be with him. The time they spent together was not always the quality time that Peter had envisioned, and sometimes, when Jimmy chose to stay home and play instead of going out, Peter felt more like a captive audience than a participant.

But over a period of weeks he realized that a significant change was taking place. Jimmy began to confide in him and sought him out with questions. When the whole family was together, Jimmy seemed more at ease, as if he felt he had a stake in both his mother and his father. And Peter, having taken the first step, found himself making more time for Jimmy not just on Saturdays but throughout the week. They were not physically together that much more, but Peter became more tuned in to Jimmy, more adept at playing with the boy on his level, and better able to read his thoughts and actions. This revitalized connection was a direct result of the changes Peter had initiated.

Because change is such a gradual process, it can be frustrating. Faced with a mountain of problems, we are tempted to take them all on at once, to try to remake lives with a single stroke of the wand. But few of us can turn around that fast. The exertion of trying usually leaves us exhausted and depressed. On the other hand, when we break the process into bite-sized pieces and accept just one at a time, we begin to move forward without even realizing it. When we reach the goal, it feels as if we've suddenly become successful, but in fact we've been building toward success, bit by bit, for a long, long time. Success does not come by accident. We make it happen, and we make it last.

10

▼

BEYOND AMBITION:
MAKING A CAREER
OF LIFE

LIKE MANY OTHERS who find themselves torn between the pressure to appear successful and the threat of internal collapse, Michael Kaufmann and Marcia Bowden were anxious to change their lives, but they weren't sure they could do it alone. Michael was referred to me by his cardiologist, who believed that Michael could prolong his life if he changed his attitudes toward competition, work, and success. Marcia came to me on her own, in the hope that therapy could save her marriage and help her find direction for herself. These two cases, with which we opened Chapter 1, were not "solved" overnight. Each required months of counseling, first to determine the adjustments that needed to be made and then to choose the best ways to implement these changes. In both cases, however, I applied the same basic strategies and principles that we have described throughout this book.

As you read the rest of Michael's and Marcia's stories, consider all that you've learned about yourself through the earlier chapters and jot down the changes you think would help *you* realize your own version of success. Then ask yourself what it would take for you to see these changes through. The most difficult question can be whether to seek professional help. Could Michael and Marcia have used this book to solve their problems on their own? In theory the answer is yes. In practice, however, Michael and Marcia, like many others who are teetering at the edge of success, were too enmeshed in their illusions and too anxious about the future to act without help. They needed the personal prodding, encouragement, and feedback that a therapist is trained to provide. Also, before they could initiate change, they had to penetrate many layers of conditioning, clarify their attitudes and values, and reassess their personal priorities. Their problems simply ran too deep to be corrected independently. So while these cases will help you better understand how you personally can act on the advice contained in this book, they may also help you determine just how close to the edge you really are. If, like Michael and Marcia, you already have one foot over the precipice, don't wait to call for professional guidance.

Michael Kaufmann

Michael's first impulse after his heart attack was to quit practicing law, take his savings, and move to a small town on a lake in Minnesota, where he could open a bait and tackle shop. He was so sure that this was the answer that he initially resisted seeking therapy. "If I switch to a simpler life and get back in touch with nature," he declared, "I'll feel great. It's all this urban competition and pressure that's making me crazy." It took some doing to persuade Michael to slow down and think things through more carefully before he acted.

Michael needed to figure out how he'd developed his attitudes toward success. The younger of two brothers, he'd been a relatively aimless youth. His brother, Harry, was not as bright as he but had a natural flair for mechanics and building, and it was always assumed that Harry would become a partner in their father's construction business when he grew up. Michael had no exceptional talents or interests as a child, although he loved to read historical chronicles and biographies.

While Michael excelled academically without much effort, he was a flop socially. Short, freckled, and slightly buck-toothed, he was shunned by the boys and teased by the girls throughout elementary school. When he was a teenager his looks improved somewhat, but his gawkiness remained. Painfully unsure of himself, he drifted from one image to another, trying to locate an identity that fit. While Harry had a tight group of friends from his shop and woodworking classes, Michael was never able to penetrate any of the cliques in his vast public high school. After a while he grew resigned to the idea that he was a nobody.

It came as a surprise to everyone, including his parents, when Michael won a scholarship to a private men's college. The family had known he was smart, of course, but his brains had never before been computed into dollars and cents. His father gave him a bear hug when he heard the news. It was Michael's first taste of competitive pride.

Michael was not by nature a competitive person. He had gotten through childhood without a single fistfight, and he had chosen cross-country running over more competitive sports. His scholarship application was the closest he'd ever come to entering a contest. Still, his parents' delighted reaction to his scholarship encouraged him to view competition in a new light.

In college Michael learned to wield logic to dominate classmates and impress professors. These tactics did not win him many friends, but they did buy him attention and a distant sort of admiration. By the end of his sophomore year his adviser was exhorting him to take pre-law courses. Michael was uncertain, but his parents urged him to follow the lead. "I never dreamed a son of mine would be a lawyer!" his mother said, beaming. "I'm always happy to have free legal advice," his father chimed in.

The decision to go into law seemed to normalize Michael's life in unexpected ways. Michael felt that he gained an identity and a role within his family. He felt relaxed, and as he let down some of his defensiveness, his social life picked up. When women heard that he was going to be a lawyer, they became attentive. Michael began to date, and by the time he entered law school he was living with a young woman who worked as a clerk in a nearby department store. By the time he graduated they were talking about marriage, and the pressure was on for Michael to get a high-paying position.

The pieces of Michael's life were falling into place, and all he had to do was stay on course. At least that's how it seemed when he first was accepted by a firm. He could already see himself as one of the firm's partners, with a big house, a pool, a well-dressed wife and kids. Then he'd really be able to thumb his nose at those school classmates who'd ridiculed him so. And think how impressed his parents would be!

Michael never anticipated the toll his profession would take on him, nor did he fully realize what was happening as his personal life gradually fell apart. He saw everyone else working late. Nobody talked much about their families or outside interests unless those interests dovetailed with those of the senior partners and could be introduced in conversation to curry favor. (Michael, for example, had developed his newfound appreciation of fishing because a senior partner had hosted a fishing expedition for the firm's more promising associates, and Michael had been included.) None of Michael's peers in the firm were married or even had steady relationships. Many of his colleagues seemed to specialize in quick, torrid affairs that provided a pleasant boost when necessary but didn't demand much time away from the office. So when Michael's girlfriend walked out on him and sixty-five-hour workweeks became routine, he took it in stride. To stay competitive he had to make certain sacrifices. It was all part of becoming a success.

After his heart attack he realized that he had to adjust his perceptions of success. Having looked back over his life, Michael knew that his plan to withdraw to some remote village would never work. He actually enjoyed having a comfortable home in the city. Admittedly, he rarely had the time or energy to take advantage of the city as he would like — for example, to go to museums or the theater — but he'd rather try to readjust his schedule than leave town. What he could not handle any longer were the pressures imposed on him by his firm. Moreover, if he was honest, he had to admit that he did not particularly want to be like the senior partners. Sure, the paycheck was attractive, but to reach the top of this particular firm you virtually had to surrender your individual identity. Whether by osmosis or design, the partners all had the same conservative politics, suburban lifestyle, fashion sensibility. Had he not had his heart attack, Michael probably would have plodded on, ending up as one of them. The thought dismayed him.

It was not law per se that was wrong; it was the track he was on and the competitive demands his firm imposed on him. It was the automatic equation of partnership with the brass ring. It was the fact that his cases weren't particularly interesting or meaningful. Michael needed to adjust his goals and rescale his life, but he didn't have to change direction entirely.

With this in mind he began to look for a new job and new sources of fulfillment outside of work. Finding a new job was a slow, tedious process, but he was excited to discover just how many options he had. True, not all of them promised a big financial payoff, but most would sustain him comfortably in his current lifestyle. And while he continued to struggle with his desire to make more money, after several months of soul searching he conceded that he was at least temporarily willing to accept a pay cut in exchange for a more balanced, more meaningful life. Finally, Michael accepted a position as counsel to a historical museum foundation. With some negotiation Michael managed to secure a good salary as well as the right to represent outside clients. But the real beauty was that in his new position, he was able to revitalize and build upon his childhood fascination with history. He achieved a sense of connection and continuity through this job that he could never have had in his old one.

Throughout his professional transition, Michael also made an effort to revitalize his private life. While recuperating from his heart attack he went back to his hometown to stay with his parents and visit with his brother. Michael's brush with mortality seemed to crystallize many of the issues that had long been rippling beneath the surface of the family, which no one had ever acknowledged. There was the competition between Michael and Harry for their parents' approval, a competition that each son believed the other had won. There were the financial worries that never seemed to cease, no matter how well their father said the construction company was doing. And there was the subtle but undeniable division between Michael, with his graduate degree, and the others, none of whom had completed more than two years of college.

The family was proud of Michael — that was evident — but they could not understand the life he led or the issues with which he was wrestling. "If I'd made the kind of dough you're making at your age," his father said more than once, "I'd have been the happiest man on earth." It did no good to point out that the money had bought Michael a heart attack and an empty life. Michael's father could not understand what he'd never known, so he was not a good source of advice. Michael's brother and mother were more sympathetic, but they too had a limited frame of reference. Come back home to live, offered his mother, and represent your father's company. We could team up and start our own company, countered his brother. Their suggestions were well-intentioned but as far off the mark as Michael's own plan to become a small-town proprietor. By the end of the visit Michael realized that he no longer had to fight for his family's approval. He had earned it and it was secure. Now it was time to develop his own priorities and instincts. At long last he was ready to accept responsibility for his own choices.

With this revelation Michael suddenly seemed to recognize needs that he had previously shoved aside in his exclusive quest for professional advancement. He saw that even if he advanced all the way to the top, that achievement alone could never make him happy. In the months that followed he began to develop a range of outside goals and activities. After years of living among packing crates and eating off paper plates, he finally furnished his home. He looked up old friends and began to construct a social life. He became active in several community organizations, which helped him to develop new relationships as well as pursue interests unconnected with his work. He joined a health club and started swimming three or four times a week. On the first anniversary of his leaving the firm, Michael celebrated by making his first commitment in years to take care of someone besides himself: he bought an aggressively affectionate Scottish terrier whom he named Mischief. Never again, Michael vowed, would he allow a job to become his sole source of responsibility or satisfaction.

In the months and years that followed, Michael often daydreamed about being a partner in a big firm, but he never seriously considered going back. His new life gave him the flexibility, fulfillment, and diversity he needed, and he was thriving on it.

Marcia Bowden

Marcia's malaise was far less focused than Michael's because it encompassed the whole family. Marcia's marriage, children, and sense of self were in jeopardy, and the problems were so entwined that Marcia didn't know where to begin. The first task in therapy, then, was to help her trace the history of her discontent.

As far as Marcia could remember, hers had been a simple childhood. She was the second of three daughters, all of whom had worked in the family store. They lived in an apartment above the store and attended the neighborhood public schools. Marcia's parents had a loving marriage that adhered to traditional role divisions. Her mother began teaching the girls to sew, cook, and keep house before they entered kindergarten. Her father was responsible for disciplining his daughters. He also dealt with all financial matters and had sole control of the family bank account. Marcia's mother never wrote a single check. Still, her parents seemed to respect and take pride in each other. If their life was not materially successful, it was filled with warmth, intimacy, and trust. Marcia associated their marital success with the way they divided family responsibilities. Growing up, she dreamed of finding a husband who could provide the wealth and status her parents had never achieved but who would treat her the way her father treated her mother. If she had that, she thought, she would have all she needed.

In Hugh, Marcia believed she'd found the answer to her dream. They fell naturally into the traditional roles of husband and wife without even considering that those roles could be modified. When Marcia's feminist friends chided her for it, Marcia snapped back, "I like knowing what's expected of me and what I can expect from Hugh. Besides, even if I wanted a job, I could never make as much as he will."

For a while their arrangement worked nicely. With financial assistance from his family, Hugh launched the first of what eventually became a chain of jewelry stores, and they rented a house nearby. Marcia worked in the store with him until their first child, Timmy, was born, when she threw herself into the duties of motherhood. By the time Hugh opened his third store and Marcia was pregnant with Patty, they were able to afford a house of their own — a white, shingled split-level with a family room and den and a quarter acre of lawn out back. Everything was going like clockwork.

Behind the scenes, however, cracks were starting to appear. The mortgage on the house and the start-up costs on the stores created a huge financial burden, and the pressure made Hugh brittle, especially at home, where Timmy was a typically rambunctious preschooler and not at all thrilled about the arrival of his baby sister. Hugh expected Marcia to keep the children under control. When, despite her best efforts, Timmy acted out or Patty refused to sleep at night, Hugh's anger bordered on violence. "I'm working too hard to put up with this," he would bellow. His fury made Marcia feel guilty and weak. While she saw the children as her primary responsibility, she was not an effective disciplinarian. She was as afraid of saying no to them as of saying no to Hugh. Patty and Timmy internalized the tension around them and condensed it into behavioral problems of their own.

Marcia began to take refuge in shopping. Having grown up without much money, she was constantly amazed by the power of the credit card. She rarely treated herself — somehow it seemed too self-indulgent to spend Hugh's money on herself — but buying things for the house, the kids, and Hugh gave her a lift when she was depressed. Admittedly the elation faded quickly, but then she could go out and buy something else. Hugh sometimes ranted over the bills when they came in, but he also liked the way Marcia kept the house and dressed the family. They were acquiring the look of prosperity, and Hugh subconsciously believed that if they kept up appearances long enough they eventually would be as successful as they looked.

As the children got older, Marcia toyed with the idea of getting a job to take some of the financial pressure off Hugh, but she was afraid he would think she was challenging his authority. She was also terrified of the independence and responsibility such a step would entail. But worst of all, she felt qualified for almost nothing but low-paying positions. And how would it reflect on the family if she went to work as a salesclerk?

Marcia and Hugh were engaged in an intricate dance of ambivalence, but neither of them realized it. Both were striving to live up to a vision of success clipped from the pages of magazines. Hugh felt it was his duty to provide the family with an impressive home and lifestyle, yet he resented having to pay the freight. He liked the idea of being the all-powerful man of the family, but as we soon discovered, he wished Marcia would show more emotional stamina and strength, not only with the children but also in their sexual relationship. Marcia, who was desperate to regain a sense of power and control over her life, was afraid the whole boat would capsize if she tried to change course.

This was where Marcia found herself at the end of our first few sessions. Having opened the dam, she had to find a way to deal with the flood of conflicts and questions pouring through. One alternative was for Hugh and Marcia to undergo marital therapy to try to attack their problems together. The other was for Marcia to plunge ahead and shake up the system on her own. The decision was made for her when Hugh refused to enter therapy, saying he was too busy. Much as this angered Marcia, it also forced her to confront her responsibility to herself. Hugh might or might not come around, but in the meantime she needed to make some changes.

Between second-guessing her husband and struggling to sustain her fantasy of the successful life, Marcia had never developed a clear picture of her own requirements for happiness. Her next step in therapy, therefore, was to visualize the experiences throughout her life that had brought her the greatest, most enduring satisfaction. Then, drawing on those experiences, she could begin to create a portrait of herself as she would like to be — not a fantasy ideal, but an image of success that integrated her talents, values, and interests as well as her needs and desires.

Over the following weeks we isolated three key areas that would have to change before she could realize her new definition of success: the balance of power and affection in her marriage; the children's behavior problems; her involvement in the family finances. Then we mapped out a series of short-term and long-term actions that could help alleviate these conflicts.

Before Marcia and Hugh could begin to work together to restore the balance in their marriage, Marcia needed to examine how she viewed herself in relation to Hugh. While her initial impulse had been to put all the blame on him as the overbearing, insensitive husband, she soon realized that she had never really challenged his attitudes or behavior. Trying to figure out why she had held herself back, Marcia saw that she had never felt like an equal partner in the marriage. Deep down she had always felt less important and less powerful than her husband. Her sense of inferiority stemmed from two basic assumptions, dating back to her childhood. One was that men — all men — were somehow more important and therefore deserved to have more authority than women. The second was that people who made a lot of money were necessarily smarter and more powerful than the rest. From the time she began dating Hugh in high school she had seen him as superior to her, first because he was a man and second because he came from a family that, while far from wealthy, had more money that her own. When he proved that he could build his stores into a prosperous chain independently, she felt even less substantial by comparison.

To redeem herself in her own eyes, Marcia needed to make a list of her own successes, accomplishments, and areas of expertise. At first her self-esteem was so badly punctured that she could find nothing positive to say about herself. So we rolled back the clock and began searching for strengths that she'd possessed in childhood, such as her loyalty to friends, her diligence and persistence in her schoolwork, and her early talent for writing and storytelling. Moving forward into her marriage, she noted that she was devoted to her family and sensitive to their problems, even though she was unable to deal with them very effectively. She also recognized that she'd succeeded in creating an attractive home and dressing her family in style.

The next step was to translate her strengths into actions that would help Marcia become more assertive, both on her own and within the marriage. She needed to communicate her feelings to Hugh and undertake more initiative in their relationship. This was no small task, considering that she had allowed, even tacitly encouraged, him to tyrannize the family. But as they began to work through their mutual misunderstandings, it became clear that Hugh had never wanted to be the dictator; he had felt, and rightly so, that Marcia expected him to call the shots.

To back down from this mandate would be a sign of weakness, in his estimation, but he had not always been certain how to make the calls and in moments of frustration had sometimes acted with undue force. While Marcia's appeal for greater authority came as something of a shock, Hugh welcomed it and encouraged her to take some of the heat off him. In particular, he revealed that he was tired of being the master in their sexual relationship and occasionally felt that he was forcing her into physical intimacy. "If you really want to be an equal partner in this relationship," he invited, "I'd like to see you show more initiative in bed." His reaction took Marcia aback and she was tempted to view it as an insult, except that Hugh was absolutely right. She had always thought Hugh would be turned off if she was sexually aggressive, but she'd never come out and asked him.

The changes Marcia and Hugh were initiating in their marriage tied directly to the other areas Marcia had targeted for improvement. The children's behavior was largely a reaction to the way she and Hugh had carved up their parenting responsibilities. They had never sat down and talked about setting and enforcing limits, and they routinely contradicted each other's rules. Because Marcia's father had always been responsible for punishing her and her sisters, Marcia accepted it as a given that Hugh should have the same job in their family, and she did not feel that she had the right to object when his punishments were overly harsh or unjustified. This was a particularly emotional issue for Marcia because it touched on all the people she loved most — her parents, her children, and her husband. Changing her behavior meant changing each of these three relationships in subtle but critical ways. First she had to separate from her parents enough to see that they were not necessarily the best models for her and Hugh. Second, she needed to work with Hugh to create a code of discipline with which they both felt comfortable. Finally, she had to become more assertive with the children, even if it meant disappointing them or making them angry with her at times.

Focusing next on the issue of family finances, Marcia realized that she and Hugh had never discussed their responsibilities in this regard either. She had always assumed that since he earned the money, he should keep track of it. But that also meant that she was completely dependent on him not only to provide the money but also to keep track of the household bills. If anything ever happened to him, or if their marriage didn't survive this period of transition, she would have no idea how their finances were organized or what it cost to keep the family afloat.

After brainstorming, Marcia decided that the short-term solution was to go over the family finances with Hugh and consider what they really needed to spend to be comfortable and happy. Could they find ways to assist their favorite charities besides giving money? Maybe they would all be better off if they took some of the money Marcia routinely spent on presents for the kids and redirected it toward an annual family vacation. If they put their money in art that they genuinely loved instead of stocks and bonds, would they get more personal satisfaction from the investment? By asking themselves these kinds of questions, Hugh and Marcia began to see how little attention they had paid to the quality of their expenditures in the past. Now it was time to put their money to work for them in a more meaningful way.

Once they'd hammered out some general guidelines, Marcia could assume a share of the accounting responsibilities. She would make a list of all their bank accounts and income sources and itemize their monthly expenses. This would give her an overview of their financial status. Then she could organize a household budget and monitor her own expenditures to stay within that budget. She could also assume the job of bill payment. Over the long term, she would track their finances and work with Hugh in overseeing their investments. These changes made Marcia feel less dependent and more like an effective partner in the marriage; they also alleviated some of the financial pressure on Hugh, making him less tense and irritable with her and the children. In addition, they helped to curb her compulsive shopping, as she transferred her zeal for spending money to the task of managing it.

As Marcia began to put these ideas into practice, the fragments of her life came together, giving her a sense of cohesiveness she could not remember ever feeling. Still, something was missing. Looking back to the portrait of herself as she would like to be, she realized that being a good wife and mother was very important to her, but she needed to do more with herself before

she could feel truly successful. After all, if her feelings of fulfillment were linked exclusively to her husband and children, what
would become of her after the children were grown? How would
she cope if Hugh died or divorced her?

She saw that shopping had provided an illusion of personal
gratification in the past. It was an activity she engaged in by
herself, one that involved decision making and judgment and
produced tangible results. But despite the quick lift shopping
gave her, Marcia took little pride in her acquisitions. She put in
the legwork, made the comparisons, selected the merchandise,
and created the look of success that pleased Hugh so much, yet
she always felt somehow disconnected from the end result. Uncomfortably aware that it was not her money and that every
choice she made had to meet with her husband's approval, Marcia never felt that she was really expressing herself. She was
merely distracting herself.

Marcia needed to bolster her career as a wife and mother with
a pursuit that satisfied her need for self-realization. "If I'm so
good at shopping, maybe I could do it professionally, as a buyer
for a store," she proposed. But while being a buyer for a store
might give her a measure of professional respectability and financial independence, Marcia quickly realized that it would give
her no more real satisfaction than being, in effect, a buyer for
Hugh and the children. Besides, the demands of employment
could well undermine the progress she was making in her relationships at home. She was not looking for escape or a source of
livelihood. She needed an occupation that would dovetail with
her domestic roles and give her a sense of independent accomplishment.

By examining her past interests and ambitions and exploring
the forms of play that most appealed to her, we found a distinct
pull toward writing. Before marrying, Marcia had sometimes
asked herself, "What if no one ever asks me to marry him and I
end up an old maid?" Her response had always been, "Well,

then I'll become a novelist and make a family of my characters." Now she saw that it had been a mistake to peg writing and family life as either-or propositions. She needed those characters every bit as much as she needed her husband and children.

Having established the direction her occupation would take, Marcia again looked for short-term and long-term plans of action. The one step she could take immediately was to start reading aggressively, everything from newspaper and magazine articles to a variety of nonfiction, novels, and children's books. As she surveyed the field, she looked for a way in — a form, a style, a readership that she could call her own. Once she had found an appropriate path, her long-term goal would, of course, be to start writing and eventually to publish her work.

It was several months before Marcia found her path. First she had to push past her daydreams about becoming a best-selling novelist or a Pulitzer Prize–winning journalist. As pleasant as those daydreams seemed, they placed such competitive pressure on the task of writing that she was immobilized. Only when she reduced her audience to herself could she begin to feel her way. Then, somewhat to her surprise, she found herself moving toward children's literature. For years she'd made up stories for Patty and Timmy and never thought anything of it. Now she wrote them down and edited them for a wider audience of children. She enlisted Hugh to help her find an illustrator, and through his advertising agency they located an artist who was delighted with the stories and willing to do the illustrations in exchange for a percentage of the profits, if and when they were able to find an interested publisher.

Of course, the process, from writing to publication, could take years, and there was no guarantee that anyone would want to publish her work, but Marcia kept reminding herself not to put too much emphasis on her first few stories. They had already served their main purpose, which was to start her writing, thinking, questioning, and stretching herself. They had entertained her children, restored her self-respect, and earned her new respect from her husband. They had given her the added sense of purpose and engagement that made her feel complete.

Finally Marcia had integrated the key elements of her life. But while clarifying her relationship with Hugh, becoming more assertive with the children, assuming greater responsibility within the household, and launching herself as a writer were all vital steps, they were only the beginning. She had to move forward, developing her relationships with Hugh and the children, developing her role in managing the household, and developing herself as a writer. For success is a process of engagement and growth as well as integration. Marcia had finally begun the process, and the future beckoned invitingly.

Moving Ahead

While Michael's and Marcia's case histories describe the broad strokes of change, they can only suggest the countless questions, fears, and choices that surround true success. As you begin to search for new directions, you won't find many fail-safe guideposts. You'll need to rely heavily on intangibles like instinct, intuition, courage, friendship, and trust. You'll need to have faith in your own abilities and potential. And you'll need to believe that you really are important, not only to yourself but to those around you.

As you prepare to do battle with your own success demons, plan your campaign loosely, giving yourself plenty of room for quick turns and impulsive maneuvers. True success cannot be controlled too tightly or it will disintegrate into boredom or frustration. To thrive, it demands a balance between spontaneity and intention, as well as between risk and certainty.

Remember that success is not a discrete experience but an open-ended process, and it therefore cannot be achieved in a single grand gesture. Rather, we create success by making sure that each and every day contains some triumph and discovery, no matter how seemingly minor or insignificant, no matter how large the opposing problems. In the end, these mundane rewards are what give us our sense of meaning, what make us feel alive and engaged in the world around us. They give us the strength to move forward, to take risks and face the unknown. They encourage us to learn from failure instead of allowing ourselves to be buried by it.

True success is analogous to the workings of a healthy mind. It incorporates our thoughts, passions, needs, and desires, and serves to organize and integrate the many skeins of daily life. At the most obvious, or conscious, level, it may focus on a single accomplishment at a time, but this focus never excludes the other vital human functions: love, friendship, caring, and contemplation. Like the mind, success has to be continually developed, expanded, and diversified. But once you grasp its power, you will know what it really means to be "somebody."

NOTES

Introduction

1. Janny Scott, "Studies Find Depression Epidemic in Young Adults," *Los Angeles Times*, October 9, 1988, 1.

Chapter 1

1. "Why We Overwork," *Los Angeles Times*, June 13, 1988, part V, 1.
2. K. Newland, *Women, Men, and the Division of Labor*, Worldwatch Paper 37 (Washington, D.C.: Worldwatch Institute, 1980).
3. "In Praise of the Conventional Life," *Forbes*, October 17, 1988, 157–158.
4. Jack Horn, "Trading Up," *Psychology Today*, October 1988, 20.
5. Ralph Waldo Emerson, "Compensation," in *Essays and English Traits* (New York: P. F. Collier and Sons, 1909), 91.

Chapter 2

1. Charles Weaver and Michael D. Matthews, *Personnel* 64, 62–65.
2. Mortimer J. Adler and William Gorman, eds. *The Great Ideas: A Synopticon of Great Books of the Western World* (Chicago: Encyclopaedia Britannica, 1952), 1043.
3. Erich Fromm, *To Have or to Be* (New York: Harper and Row, 1976), 82.
4. Ibid., 36.
5. Aristotle, "Nicomachean Ethics," in *The Basic Works of Aristotle*, ed. Richard McKean (New York: Random House, 1941), 937.

Chapter 3

1. Ann Moseley, "School Blues: The Secret Stress Life of Your Child," *Child*, September 1988, 98.

Chapter 4

1. Howard Taubman, *Music on My Beat* (New York: Simon and Schuster, 1943).
2. Ann Moseley, "School Blues: The Secret Stress Life of Your Child," *Child*, September 1988, 98.
3. James Block, ed., *Mastery Learning: Theory and Practice* (New York: Holt, Rinehart and Winston, 1971), 47.
4. Ibid., 19.
5. Ibid., 8.
6. Wilbur B. Brookover, Thomas Shailer, and Ann Paterson, "Self-Concept of Ability and School Achievement," *Sociology of Education* 37 (1964): 271–278.
7. Erich Fromm, *To Have or to Be* (New York: Harper and Row, 1976), 6.
8. Elizabeth Stark, "Wild Blue Blunders," *Psychology Today*, October 1988, 30.
9. David Johnson and Roger Johnson, "The Socialization and Achievement Crisis: Are Cooperative Learning Experiences the Solution?" *Applied Sociology Annual 4*, ed. L. Bickman. (Beverly Hills: Sage Publications, 1983), 146.

Chapter 5

1. Fleming Meeks, "Life Experience versus Case Studies," *Forbes*, October 3, 1988, 188.
2. John Byrne, "Let's Hear It for Liberal Arts," *Forbes*, July 1, 1985, 112.
3. Srully Blotnick, *Otherwise Engaged* (New York: Facts on File, 1985).
4. Paul Hawken, *The Next Economy* (New York: Holt, Rinehart and Winston, 1983), 162.
5. Alvin Toffler, *The Third Wave* (New York: William Morrow, 1980), 66.
6. Mitchell Marks, "The Disappearing Company Man," *Psychology Today*, September 1988, 34–39.
7. Srully Blotnick, *The Corporate Steeplechase* (New York: Facts on File, 1984).

Chapter 6

1. Pauline Sears, "Levels of Aspiration in Academically Successful and Unsuccessful Children," *Journal of Abnormal Social Psychology* 35 (1940): 498–536.

2. Srully Blotnick, *The Corporate Steeplechase* (New York: Facts on File, 1984), 20.
3. Jeff Meer, "Will the Real Impostor Please Stand Up?" *Psychology Today*, April 1985, 24–25.
4. Joseph Epstein, *Ambition: The Secret Passion* (New York: E. P. Dutton, 1980), 226.

Chapter 7

1. Juanita Williams, *Psychology of Women* (New York: W. W. Norton, 1987), 369.
2. U.S. Bureau of Labor Statistics, unpublished data.
3. Kathleen Gerson, "Briefcase, Baby, or Both?" *Psychology Today*, November 1986, 30–36.
4. Williams, *Psychology*, 221–225.
5. Margaret Hennig and Anne Jardim, *The Managerial Woman* (New York: Anchor/Doubleday, 1977), 13–14.
6. Ibid.
7. *The World Almanac and Book of Facts*, 1988, 86.
8. Nicole Yorkin, "On the Job," *Los Angeles Times Magazine*, December 4, 1988, 22.
9. "Executive Women: Substance Plus Style," *Psychology Today*, August 1987, 18–26.
10. Kathryn Stechart, *Sweet Success* (New York: Macmillan, 1986), 163.
11. Ibid., 165.
12. E. E. Maccoby and C. Jacklin, *The Psychology of Sex Differences* (Stanford: Stanford University Press, 1974).
13. Stechart, *Success*, 123.
14. J. P. Lemkau, "Personality and Background Characteristics of Women in Male-dominated Occupations: A Review," *Psychology of Women Quarterly* 4 (1979): 221–240.
15. Margaret Hennig, "Family Dynamics and the Successful Woman Executive," in R. Knudsin, ed., *Women and Success* (New York: William Morrow, 1973).
16. M. E. Tidball, "Women's Colleges and Women Achievers Revisited," *Signs: Journal of Women in Culture and Society* 5 (1980): 504–507.
17. Yorkin, "On the Job," 18–24.
18. Anita Shreve, "Fast-Lane Kids," *New York Times Magazine*, June 12, 1988, 50–57.
19. Robert Atkinson, *The Teenage World: Adolescent Self-Image in Ten Countries* (New York: Plenum Press, 1988).

20. Margaret Mead, *Sex and Temperament in Three Primitive Societies* (New York: William Morrow, 1935).
21. Janet Hyde and B. G. Rosenberg, *Half the Human Experience* (Lexington, Mass.: D. C. Heath, 1976), 358.

Chapter 8

1. Charles Kaiser, "The Wages of Greed," *Lear's*, November 1988, 39–40.
2. "In Praise of the Conventional Life," *Forbes*, October 17, 1988, 157–158.
3. Erich Fromm, *To Have or to Be* (New York: Harper and Row, 1976), 148.
4. Allan Luks, "Helper's High," *Psychology Today*, October 1988, 39–42.
5. Gilbert Brim, "Losing and Winning," *Psychology Today*, September 1988, 48.
6. Lee Iacocca with William Novak, *Iacocca: An Autobiography* (New York: Bantam Books, 1984), 43.

Chapter 9

1. Mortimer J. Adler and William Gorman, eds., *The Great Ideas: A Synopticon of Great Books of the Western World* (Chicago: Encyclopaedia Britannica, 1952), 921.
2. Dennis Wholey, *Discovering Happiness* (New York: Avon Books, 1988), 266.
3. Judith Rodin and Peter Salovey, in *Journal of Social and Clinical Psychology*, November 1988.
4. Patricia Dreyfuss, "Investing: The Profits of Conscience," *Lear's*, November, 1988, 47.